PENGUIN BOOKS

My Italians

oberto Saviano was born in Naples in 1979. He is the author of
Rhe international bestseller *Gomorrah*, the film adaptation of
tlwhich won the Grand Prix of the 2008 Cannes Film Festival, and
Zero Zero Zero. He has been living under police protection since
October 2006, following threats received from the criminal
organizations that he denounced. In November 2008 Saviano was
invited by the Nobel Committee in Stockholm to give a lecture
on 'Freedom of Speech and Lawless Violence'.

My Italians

True Stories of Crime and Courage

ROBERTO SAVIANO

Translated by Anne Milano Appel

PENGUIN BOOKS

PENGUIN BOOKS

UK | USA | Canada | Ireland | Australia
India | New Zealand | South Africa

Penguin Books is part of the Penguin Random House group of companies
whose addresses can be found at global.penguinrandomhouse.com.

Penguin
Random House
UK

First published in Italian, under the title *Vieni via con me*, by Feltrinelli Editore, Milan, 2010
This translation first published 2016

001

Published by arrangement with Agenzia Letteraria Roberto Santachiara

The extract from Gabriel García Márquez's *One Hundred Years of Solitude* on p. 54 is from the
Harper Perennial Modern Classics edition (2006), translated by Gregory Rabassa, p. 17.

Set in 11/13pt Dante MT Std
Typeset by Palimpsest Book Production Ltd, Falkirk, Stirlingshire
Printed in Great Britain by Clays Ltd, St Ives plc

A CIP catalogue record for this book is available from the British Library

ISBN: 978-1-846-14704-3

www.greenpenguin.co.uk

MIX
Paper from
responsible sources
FSC
www.fsc.org   FSC® C018179

Penguin Random House is committed to a
sustainable future for our business, our readers
and our planet. This book is made from Forest
Stewardship Council® certified paper.

Contents

CONTENTS

Preface

For a writer there is something unreal about working on a television show and putting it together from start to finish. On the page, everything you write leaves room for imagination; everything you recount can be experienced, pondered and elaborated upon in the reader's mind and soul. With television that's not the case: with television the words are not written down – you have to visualize the words. A narrative is most effective when you don't try to faithfully reproduce life, but instead transform it truthfully into a story. In essence if you're a writer you feel out of place everywhere but on the page, and yet when I was invited to tell stories about Italy on television, my answer was instinctively 'yes'. I was excited about it, but I could only nod my head briefly, as if it were my body saying 'yes' rather than my brain.

And so an adventure began, made up of tension, sorrow and intense passion, an adventure that made me giddy and afforded me a chance to glimpse a way out of the dark night. The night of my country. I was dreaming of an ambitious, quality programme, with prominent guests: a show intended for a wide audience, that would portray an Italy rarely shown on TV. I wanted to talk about the mudslinging machine, the systematic process of discrediting people who speak out, about the mafia and politics, about how vote-buying works, about the lies surrounding the earthquake of L'Aquila, about the waste-disposal business. My dream (or ambition) was to speak to that segment of the country that is actually the largest, the part that wants to redesign the nation and rebuild it, that wants to declare that all Italians are not the same and that our diversity lies in being able to make mistakes without being corrupt, in having weaknesses that do not involve blackmail and extortion. I wanted to speak to that portion of the population that dreams, unashamedly, of being able to call this land of ours, which today is so forlorn, their country, *patria*, once again.

The resulting programme was aired in 2010 in four episodes and was called *Vieni via con me* (*Come Away With Me*). My TV monologues form the basis for the chapters in this book. The series was a sort of TV revolution: aired on Raitre (the third national channel) against the will of and with no support from the network's highest executives. Despised by the government, it became a huge public success, the most viewed programme in the history of Raitre.

'To see what is in front of one's nose,' George Orwell wrote, 'needs a constant struggle.' More than five years have passed since the series was aired, and after three successive governments there remains a certainty: nothing has really changed. Or better, what remains is a sense of impotence: now that Silvio Berlusconi is not presiding over Italy any more, now that we have a new, young and left-wing government, we are silenced by hope and disappointed by reality.

Even if some parts of the mudslinging machine appear to have been dismantled, it continues to operate, silently, ready to spring into action whenever it is needed. Worse still, there has been absolutely no progress in terms of the fundamental legislation that would strengthen Italy's democracy. A natural disaster can still offer a good opportunity to those who want to siphon off public money, and key civil rights, like the recognition of same-sex unions and laws regarding the end of life, are still not guaranteed. As such, this book is as representative of Italy today as it was five years ago. The *Lega Nord* continues to exert considerable political pressure, and the government lacks the unity and strength to implement the reforms that the country really needs. Italy remains a two-speed country: the North attracts most of the investment and the South, lacking in infrastructure, is left to the most dangerous of enterprises: criminal organizations.

That's the reason why I considered (and consider) it essential to commemorate the epic of national unification, which was motivated by ideals, not just economic interests, based on a federalism of solidarity rather than a self-seeking federalism like the one the *Lega Nord* appeals to today. A movement which started in the South, an area torn by criminal organizations, a mirror of our entire country: a hush-up which seems more and more difficult to come to terms with. It's been very difficult to talk about the North as a terrain invaded by the South's mafia, because it is not easy to accept the idea that a large part of the Italian economy is determined in unfamiliar, backward southern villages rather than in the big, modern northern metropolises. The bandit Salvatore Giuliano used to say: '*In città scivolo*,' in the city I can slip, meaning that your footing is steady on soil, whereas on pavement, in the cities, where everyone is unfamiliar, you can become disoriented and you're likely to make mistakes. Platì, Casal di Principe, Africo, Corleone, Casapesenna, Natile Careri: these are the places from which most of Italy's capital is controlled. It is here, in the villages, that rules are written and administered. Though they are economic rules, they are first and foremost cultural, and they reach as far as the cities, even in the North or all the way to Germany, as demonstrated by the Duisburg massacre in the summer of 2007. The same affiliation rites that are believed to pertain only to backward regions are replicated even in the North; identical rituals are performed in response to the same immutable code. It's not just militant dynamics, but primarily cultural dynamics that are nurtured by practices that are atavistic, perennial, fixed, eternal. Rules adopted as a way of life, as a mechanism for being in the world. Rules that are the force behind Italy's most powerful entrepreneurial factions: the 'Ndrangheta, the Camorra and the Cosa Nostra. It would be too simple to believe that all this is the result of medieval backwardness, profound ignorance and the absence of the State. Because there is no backwardness in a place where millions and millions of Euros flow in through drug trafficking. That's precisely the crux of the matter: the highest degree of traditional archaic rule, combined with the highest degree of economic development. The Web, the market, finance, drugs, yet all governed by the rules of property, of downcast eyes, of arranged marriages, of virginity and blood.

I didn't want to tell stories about a backward village in the South in the hands of Mafia families. Many of the millions of viewers who watched us would have perceived them as remote, unrelated to them: stories that would not have had the power to engage the whole country. So I decided to talk about what was happening in the North, in Lombardy, in cement, in the drug trade, in the distribution of food and gas, in contract management, in the influences on local governments. I wanted to report what happens in the healthcare sector in Monza, in Novara, in the towns of Giussano, Seregno, Verano Brianza, Mariano Comense, Desio. These are not marginal stories, as they would have you believe. They are stories that concern everyone, the result of a system that is obeyed by those who at this time control much of my beautiful, ill-fated country. Yet my reconstruction of the Mafia's infiltration in Lombardy, territory of the *Lega Nord*, was described as 'infamous'. 'For Saviano, the North is trash,' they wrote in the papers, 'For Saviano, the North is Mafia-run,' simplifying to the utmost what I had presented in the broadcast, beginning with investigations into the infiltration of criminal organizations in the North and with the Legambiente's reports on the *ecomafia*. As often happens, it's as if the one telling the facts were at fault, the one exposing the mechanisms, the one who recalls the past asking the nation to face the findings as a unified front. The word that generated such an uproar in those days is '*interloquire*', to have a say in. I had stated that the Mafia organizations have a say in discussions with political powers and that in the North, where political power is in the hands of the *Lega Nord*, the 'Ndrangheta chimes in with the League. I had based this on investigations which report continuous attempts by the 'Ndrangheta to influence the lists of candidates, and which describe intercepted communications among 'Ndrangheta members who speak of the League to one another as a party that they can influence, approach, control. '*Interloquire*': a very broad term which does not by any means establish direct collusion or corruption, but which is a premise for suggesting that no one can feel safe and that no areas are immune from criminal money and the mafia-entrepreneurial alliance. Many politicians have even exploited the love story between Piergiorgio and Mina Welby (the first being affected by amyotrophic lateral sclerosis, they both fought to grant Piergiorgio a dignified death without the assistance of a breathing machine) and the testimony of Beppino Englaro (father of Eluana Englaro, a woman who, after a car crash, has lived for seventeen years in a vegetative state) in the debate about the right to die. They tried to build consensus by discrediting people who gave strength and meaning to Italian institutions. 'The good man will act only on maxims which he can at the same time will to be universal laws': in the affairs of Beppino, Piergiorgio and Mina this Kantian principle was informed with blood, sweat and tears. And a defence of rights. Refusing to take a quicker way out, Beppino, Piergiorgio and Mina asked the institutions of our country for civility, understanding and the respect of a judgment from the Court of Cassation. They could have left Italy but they didn't do so, turning their bodies into the battleground for a crusade in defence of fundamental human rights, in order to confirm the inalienable right of every individual to be able to freely decide on the type of care they undergo: treatment which is considered a cure and that involves keeping a patient alive at all costs.

Maybe it's only when faced with such evidence that we are able to explain the story of Socrates, to understand, after having heard it thousands of times, why he drank the hemlock rather than running away. A way out that is not taken, that is actually abhorrent, is much more than a campaign in favour of a single dignified death: it is a battle in defence of every individual's life. The daily struggle of Beppino, Mina and Piergiorgio was a struggle in defence of rights, because it is clear that the essence of the law is the right to live. By acting as they did, they led the way to a new approach, showing that a person can and should remain in Italy, using the tools that democracy provides. For once, conscience and the law did not emigrate from our country. For once, people did not leave in order to obtain or even just ask for something, no attempt was made to be heard elsewhere. No Italian citizen, whatever he may think, can refuse to respect Beppino Englaro, who requested that a judgment of the Court of Cassation be applied, and Mina Welby, who fought for her Piero to have a Catholic funeral: two citizens whose actions restored to our country the dignity that often we ourselves take away.

In the days following the broadcast they called us the 'death party', in contrast to the 'life party'. They simplified religion and politics, making them into a battleground without considering the fact that we portrayed a church which, in Italy, out of the spotlight, is the only one operating in the most difficult areas, in the most desperate situations, the only one that affords human dignity to migrants, to those the institutions overlook, to those who can't stay afloat in the crisis. It would be nice if the ending of this story could be that in Italy, tomorrow, thanks to the non-violent battle of Beppino, Piergiorgio and Mina, each of us would be free to choose: to be kept alive by machines in a vegetative state for decades or elect our own end without having to emigrate. Just as patients in a permanent comatose state choosing to continue the support should be afforded decent, ongoing assistance without having to be a burden on the families, as often happens. This is an Italy that would embrace rights and compassion, that would allow choices different from one's own to be respected and understood, an Italy with which it would be wonderful to be able to identify. Wanting to see yourself in a country that's different, starting from where you feel the story pertains to you, where that idea of life pertains to you. Getting angry about the filth to which power often forces you: the shamefulness of it.

Like the many Neapolitans who have had enough of being constantly described as overflowing with trash, hurt by seeing their city covered with garbage. 'Because we believed Berlusconi, and now how do we get out of it?' 'I knew the garbage would come back and that Berlusconi hadn't solved anything. That's politics.' Those are the first two comments (their simplicity makes me smile) made by a listener who calls in to a local radio station which gives Neapolitans a chance to vent their outrage after an avalanche of refuse has once again, for the umpteenth time, inundated the streets of the city. Everything, periodically, goes back to the way it was before. But in Naples, almost as if to ward off bad luck, you can no longer talk about the waste crisis and you should not even mention the so called 'land of fires' of which I wrote in my first book, *Gomorrah* – that triangle of land poisoned by decades of illegal and dangerous waste traffic and never reclaimed. Every now and then the city centre goes back to stinking like a garbage dump, the streets are lined with trash again, the population continues to protest against the opening of new landfills, alarmed that they might attract not only lawful refuse but also illegal waste, as Campania's landfills have always done. Sometimes they're lucky enough, when nothing happens in the world to monopolize attention, and the news is heard; at other times there's a hurricane, a plane crash, a flood, or a sex scandal, and the protests are passed over in silence. They try to say that the soil is safe, that only a small amount of it is polluted, but waste continues to burn, the air in these areas is almost unbreathable, people die of cancer and no answer seems to be due. Governments change, but they keep on telling us: 'You see? Everything is fine, the citizens' committees that were protesting earlier have realized that the landfills are harmless and necessary.'

False. But after years of sticking-plaster solutions that have done nothing to solve the problem, this enormous sham is sometimes exposed, sometimes not, and it's the region and the people's health that pay the price. Landfills are overflowing because they've been filled, in recent decades, with all types of waste from outside the region. But if you report this you get an immediate, violent reaction from the mayors of the municipalities you mention: those from which the toxic wastes came and those in which the wastes were spilled, entombed, buried or hidden. All threatening lawsuits simply because you stated that those areas are toxic-waste trafficking zones. The Camorra continues to profit in all of this, while the lack of solidarity on the part of some regions of the North – which refused to accept Campania's waste when needed so that the cycle might be normalized – has proved to be once again a short-sighted, perhaps unwitting, gift to the clans.

Telling the story does not change what happened, but it can alter what is to come. That's the power of the narrative: when a story is heard, it becomes part of those who feel it's their own and then act on what hasn't yet happened. Every story has this margin of uncertainty, which resides in the perception of the listener. Hearing a story and feeling that it relates to you is like acquiring a formula to fix the world. I often think of a story the way a virologist does a virus, because a story can also become a contagious form which, by transforming people, transforms the world itself.

The Italy that listened to those monologues moved me. Each day I received thousands of letters and messages from people attesting to their receptiveness, their solidarity. Men and women who wanted to share their approval, as if a fresh breeze had begun to blow. What suffused every part of me during that time was actually the feeling that through that medium, television, which often seems useless, a device for obscuring people's minds, a desire was building up: a longing to transform, to change, to speak out polit-ically, to show that the country is different from the way it is portrayed, different from its political class, different from the cri-sis that it is going through.

The initial challenge was to portray this different Italy through 'lists' that would be the programme's framework and grammar. A simple idea, because lists are containers for everything, every experience, every story. Here, too, audience participation was at a high: everyone thought of his or her own list, and during the broadcast, via Facebook and the website, thousands of them came in. Beautiful, funny, dramatic. I was reminded of the scene in the film *Manhattan*, when Woody Allen, lying on the couch, reflects on 'An idea for a short story about, um, people in Man-hattan who are constantly creating these real, unnecessary, neurotic problems for themselves 'cos it keeps them from dealing with more unsolvable, terrifying problems about ... the universe.' As an antidote, Allen thinks of something optimistic: a list of things that make life worthwhile. Of course it's an expedient, the chronically ill person is him, and the optimistic list is useful to him and him alone, to free him from the pointless, neurotic issues which hold him captive. Woody Allen lists Groucho Marx, Willie Mays, the second movement of Mozart's *Jupiter* Symphony, Louis Armstrong, Flaubert's *Sentimental Education*, Swedish films, Mar-lon Brando, Frank Sinatra, those incredible apples and pears painted by Cézanne, the crabs at Sam Wo's and Tracy's face. A light-hearted list that is worth more than a moral compass for those at a loss.

I've always been attracted to lists. Someday I'd like to write books of lists. And I'm confident that a list of things that make life worth living is a fundamental exercise for remembering what we're made of. A map of ourselves. I would like to spend my time seeing what people write, the ten things that give meaning to their lives. I would have liked to read them all on the air. But on television words must always be used sparingly.

Here, however, I have paper in front of me, it never limits me. Unfortunately and fortunately. This is my list. These are the ten things which, for me, make life worthwhile:

1) *Mozzarella di bufala* from Aversa.
2) Bill Evans playing the 'Love Theme from *Spartacus*'.
3) Going to the tomb of Raffaello Sanzio with the person you love most and reading the Latin inscription which many are unaware of.
4) Maradona's 2-0 goal against England at the 1986 World Cup in Mexico (my apologies!).
5) The *Iliad*.
6) Listening to Bob Marley singing 'Redemption Song' in your earbuds while walking along, free.
7) Diving, but out in the deep, where the sea is the sea.
8) Dreaming of returning home after you've been forced to stay away a long, long time.
9) Making love on a summer afternoon. In the South of Italy.
10) Turning on the computer after a day when they've collected signatures against you and finding an email from your brother that says: 'I'm proud of you.'

I Swear

I hold in my hands an Italian flag. The first Italian flag, even before they sewed the Savoy shield in the centre. I like to feel it between my fingers because I think it is something more than a symbol. All flags are symbols, symbols with which people identify. But this flag is not just a symbol, an object whose function is to represent the nation's unity. I like to keep in mind, especially as someone who comes from the South, that this flag also represents the idea of a nation engendered by a dream. It is the sign of a dream. Behind the bloodshed, the insurrections, the protagonists and other names, the dates, we Italians have a legacy: unlike what took place in Spain, France and Germany, the unification of Italy was a dream, not simply a plan, not just a pact among aristocrats. In the mind of Giuseppe Mazzini, in the work of Carlo Pisacane, in the dream of hundreds and thousands of republican thinkers, of *unitaristi*, those who supported unification, a united Italy was not simply the union of geographically related regions, nor, as in the case of other countries, an accord among the aristocracy or other power groups. In the minds of those men, the unification of Italy was the only way to free the Italian people from injustice, after three centuries of foreign domination. The tactic could only be that of unity, which is why for them that flag came to symbolize the possibility of being emancipated from suffering, poverty and injustice. That was their dream.

It is obvious that the idiotic nonsense we've been listening to in recent years, which contends that splitting the country would be a way to make it stronger, is not only short-sighted but also historically unsustainable. If we look at a map of Italy before uni-fication, the Kingdom of Sardinia, the Savoy realm, would be a small sovereignty bordering France. And what else would Lombardy-Veneto be, if not an appendage of Austria? And the Papal State at the centre? A symbolic state. Without the unifica-tion of Italy we would go back to being someone's marginal accessory, even today. The centrality and unity of the nation had a different aspiration, a different design: 'We will determine our own destiny.' Those who now think they can split the country up are only going backwards, weakening us, destroying what had been a magnificent dream: the possibility of shaping a different destiny, the dream of being able to see Friuli and Calabria united through a single language, a single blood, a single homeland.

At the beginning of the unification process the hope was that Italy could become emancipated on its own, without the aid of foreign powers. It was thought that the South – the region far-thest away from the Austrian garrisons of Lombardy-Veneto – was the place from which the push for a united, republican Italy might start. Among other things, Italy's only real Jacobin revolution had occurred in Naples in 1799. The ideals of the French Revolution had spread from Naples: Antonio Genovesi, Gaetano Filangieri and the abbot Galiani had inspired French revolutionaries from Marat to Danton. Not surprisingly, three Neapolitan Jacobins are considered the first martyrs of the Risorgimento: Vitaliani, Galiani and De Deo.

In addition, I often recall the Calabrian martyrs Michele Bello, Rocco Verduci, Gaetano Ruffo, Domenico Salvadori and Pietro Mazzoni. They ranged in age from twenty-three to twenty-eight years old. They were all educated in Naples, where they had stud-ied law. Verduci's grandfather was one of the founders of the Neapolitan Republic.

They are five names that are nearly unknown, five young men who died in their early twenties for the dream of creating a united Italy, of unifying it starting from the South. They are the martyrs of Gerace, where they were sentenced to death on 1 October 1847 for having led the revolt which had ignited the area in the early days of September. The sentence was carried out the following day, and as a sign of contempt the bodies of the five patriots were thrown into a mass grave known as '*la lupa*', the 'wolf'. The brief trial that resulted in the convictions was perfunctory, already pre-decided, unless one of the men was willing to be an informer and reveal the names of other insurgents. No one informed, however. Just as many others – boys, young men – did not inform, but committed suicide in prison rather than become traitors. Some-times the police, accompanying the condemned man to the gallows, would even make him pass under the windows of his house in an extreme attempt to make him talk, to make him name his comrades in exchange for his life. Andrea Vochieri, a lawyer from Alessandria, and Amatore Sciesa, a Milanese up-holsterer, are just two of the names of those who did not yield; when led past his house, Sciesa told the police '*Tiremm' innanz'* (keep going).

It is not realistic to think that splitting up the country is the solution to its current problems. The continuity with those ear-lier ideals lies instead in thinking that we are better than our political class, that the nation wants to be restructured, that it wants to act, that its talents want to emerge at long last, that we should stop assuming that the best finish last and learn to dream that the best will finish first. That means dreaming with the ideal-istic aspirations held by the *unitaristi*. Embracing the idea of being able to construct this Italy means being true heirs of the thinking behind Italian Unity.

It's the opposite of the load of bullshit the *Lega Nord* spouts when it claims that the South is a burden on the North. Or when, for example, it names a research institution after one of the lead-ing thinkers and patriots of the Risorgimento, Carlo Cattaneo. The charge of the Friends of Carlo Cattaneo Foundation – founded in Besozzo, in the province of Varese, whose honorary president is Senator Umberto Bossi, former leader of the *Lega Nord* – is to re-examine the unpublished documents produced by Cattaneo during his exile in the Swiss village of Castagnola, on the northern shore of Lake Lugano, between 1848 and 1869. However, the Italian federalist tradition that Cattaneo began is quite the opposite of the self-interested federalism of the *Lega Nord*. Cattaneo's federalism was one of solidarity, which established an association between the citizens' welfare and self-government. His models were the Swiss Confederation and the United States: for him, small town councils and autonomous local government were the 'backbone' of the nation and constituted 'the nation in the innermost bastion of its freedom'. Not even when Italy was born in 1861, monarchist and centralist, not even at that time did the republican and federalist Cattaneo dream of talking about secession.

I am perhaps privileged since I am the son of a Neapolitan father and a mother of Ligurian origin. I have the blood of the South and the blood of the North in me. I grew up with my grandfather Carlo's memories of Mazzini and my grandfather Stefano's stories of brigands. Often my ancestors paid for those ideals of theirs. But handed down to me from my family's oral tradition, like a lullaby, was the oath that young men took when they became members of Young Italy. I like to remember it because the words contain the commitment, the dream and the sacrifice of the young people who created Italy, whose names cannot be obliterated by cries for secession, by ostentation, by the concept of Padania and green shirts. And by the egotism of those who believe that Unity is a detriment rather than a benefit to all:

> I give my name to Young Italy, an association of men holding the same faith … This I do swear, invoking upon my head the wrath of God, the abhorrence of man, and the infamy of the perjurer, if I ever betray the whole or a part of this my oath.

I Swear

I swear to obey all the instructions, in conformity with the spirit of Young Italy, given me by those who represent with me the union of my Italian brothers; and to keep secret these instructions, even at the cost of my life. I swear to dedicate myself wholly and forever to endeavour with them to constitute Italy as a single, free, independent, republican nation.

The 'Ndrangheta in the North

The story goes that around 1412 three Spanish knights, Osso, Mastrosso and Carcagnosso, who belonged to a secret society in Toledo, escaped from Spain after having avenged with blood the honour of a sister raped by an arrogant nobleman. They boarded a ship and reached Favignana, off the coast of Trapani, a perfect island to hide on given its many grottoes. They remained there for twenty-nine years, hidden in the bowels of the earth, but over this long period of time they applied themselves to defining the codes that were to be kept secret from the eyes of the uninitiated and which would become the 'tablets of the law' of a secret society similar to Garduña, the secret criminal organization that they had had to leave hastily and which was particularly active in Spain starting in the fifteenth century. The three knights thus established the rules for future mafia generations and, when they left their caves, began their mission of proselytizing. Osso, the laziest one, stopped in Sicily and founded the Mafia; Mastrosso crossed the Strait of Messina, went to Calabria and established the 'Ndrangheta; Carcagnosso, the most enterprising, reached the capital of the Kingdom, Naples, after an adventurous journey and there he instituted the Camorra.

It's only a legend, of course, a fable easy to grasp and remember, deliberately devised to pass the time during long days in prison. Moreover, it is in the prisons that the *picciotti*, mafia footsoldiers, telling stories about knights and conquests, could continue their proselytizing and find new disciples, following the tradition of Osso, Mastrosso and Carcagnosso. Being a knight involved identifying with an ideology, obeying a code of rules founded on courage, loyalty, keeping one's word and a sense of belonging. A set of values that can be summed up in a single word, still used and abused today: honour. The knight was first and foremost a man of honour.

It may seem paradoxical that the mafias in Italy, the country par excellence when it comes to not having rules, have more rules than international mafias. Italy produces a disciplined mafia. Criminal organizations should not be viewed as confused structures, where different interests roam the marketplace like gangsters in search of loot and money. Unfortunately it is not so simple, in fact in the areas of drug trafficking, of investment, where the only objective is gain, the Italian mafias display a distinctive trait: the reliability of the organization.

It is interesting to understand the symbolic way an *affiliato*, an associate, is taken into an organization such as the Cosa Nostra, the Camorra or the 'Ndrangheta. When he becomes part of a criminal organization, he enters it through symbolic rituals, baptisms, because the criminal structures are true hierarchical organizations with classifications, rituals, wages, responsibilities. Being part of a criminal organization means being part of a structure that in some ways resembles a corporation, in some ways a religious order, and in some ways an ancient army (like the Roman army, which was made up of legions).

For example, the person to be 'baptized' in the 'Ndrangheta, the one who is about to become an associate, has a name: he is called the '*contrasto onorato*'. In the 'Ndrangheta's lingo, general members of the public are '*contrasti*', and those who respect the Mafia and do not oppose it are called '*contrasti onorati*'. But they are not yet '*affiliati*', or associates. One reaches the first level of actual affiliation, namely '*picciotto d'onore*', honourable young soldier, through an atavistic ritual, identical for all time. The associates take their places in a room, around a u-shaped table – no one really knows why, but that's how it is – then the *capo-società*, an elder of the organization and chairman of the meeting, reads out a very long rite; afterwards the initiate takes an oath and assumes the responsibility for being part of an organization whose code will stand above his family, his children, his own blood. The 'Ndranghetisti call each other 'blood brothers', because a blood brother is one whom you choose; a biological brother on the other hand is the brother of sin, because to give birth to him the mother committed a sin with the father.

It seems incredible, but even today there are young people in Italy who live according to the course of action prescribed by this oath. Outside the organizations, it is a rite known only to scholars and magistrates:

ELDER: Good evening, learned associates.

ASSOCIATES: Good evening.

ELDER: In the name of our ancient ancestors, the three Spanish knights Osso, Mastrosso and Carcagnosso, I baptize this place. If earlier I identified it as a place where cops and felons gather, from now on I will recognize it as a holy and inviolable place where this honoured society can form and transform. Do you conform?

A: We conform.

ELDER: To what?

A: To the rules of the society.

ELDER: In the name of the Archangel Gabriel and Saint Elizabeth, the circle of society is formed. What is said in this u-shaped circle is said here and stays here, anyone who speaks outside this place is declared a traitor to his office and discharged from this society. We are gathered here to initiate a *contrasto onorato* who has distinguished himself for his virtue and humility, his guarantor is [here the name of the person who vouches for the introduction is spoken]. If anyone present has any objections, say so now or forever hold your peace. You may introduce the *honourable man* [the guarantor introduces the person to the Elder]: who are you and what do you want?

NEW ASSOCIATE: My name is [first and last name] and I seek blood and honour.

ELDER: Blood for whom?

NA: For the wicked.

ELDER: Honour for whom?

NA: For the Honoured Society.

ELDER: Are you familiar with our rules?

NA: I am familiar with them.

ELDER: The interest or honour of the society comes before family, parents, sisters or brothers; from this moment on, the society is your family, and if you commit infamy you will be punished by death. Just as you will be loyal to the society, so the society will be loyal to you and will assist you in need; this oath can be broken only by death. Are you prepared for this? Do you so swear?

[The new associate places his left hand, palm facing down, on the tip of a knife held by one of the participants, while the others present place their left hand on that of the initiate.]

NA: I swear in the name of the archangel Gabriel and the Sacred Crown of the Honoured Society, that from this time on you are my family, that I will always be loyal and that only death will take me from you; I place myself in your hands, that you may judge me should I commit acts or offences that may be detrimental to the clan, staining my honour or that of others, and that may cause harm to the Honoured Society; if I commit a wrong I will be punished with death.

[The capo-società places his left hand over all the others.]

ELDER: If at first I knew you as a *contrasto onorato*, from now on I recognize you as a *picciotto d'onore* (honourable soldier).

[The new associate gives the Elder three kisses on the cheek.]

[At the completion of the rite, the Elder turns to the formed circle and recites the formula that ends the meeting of the society.]

ELDER: From this moment on we have a new man of honour,

the Society has been formed, and the circle is dismissed. Good evening.

A: Good evening.

They are the words of a terrible marriage that can only be dissolved by death.

When they are in Aspromonte, in Polsi, a district of San Luca, in the province of Reggio Calabria, the oath takes place under a tree, the tree of knowledge, which is located in a gorge. The 'Ndrangheta has always met and sworn in front of this tree. Once I went inside it; it's an old chestnut tree with a hollow trunk. The tree represents the hierarchy of the 'Ndranghetisti: trunk, limbs, branches, twigs, flowers and leaves. The leaves, which fall and rot on the ground, represent infamous traitors who betray the organization.

The hierarchies are critical because they are the foundation of the code. The Italian mafias are conservative, traditionalist. The American families on the other hand have become modernized, emancipated. Joe Pistone, the famous Donnie Brasco, says that during the six years he was infiltrated in the Bonanno family, one of the five New York families, he realized that the more Americanized the mafiosi became, the more heavy-handed they were: they didn't understand that you don't commit a crime only to get rich, that if you violate the code you also go against the mafia way of life. When they needed to be strengthened again, according to Donnie Brasco, the American families sent for the Italians, who restored hierarchy, discipline, structure. It may seem paradoxical, but it is not. In the 1970s, Vincenzo Macrì, grandson and designated heir of Antonio Macrì, boss of the Siderno family in Locride, was 'laid to rest' (that is, ousted from the organization) because his attitudes were not considered to be consistent with those of a good 'Ndranghetista: Vincenzo rode a Vespa, went around in T-shirts and shorts. So he was 'put to rest' and one of the Comissos of Siderno was appointed family boss in his place. Even today an 'Ndranghetista must adhere strictly to certain criteria: he must not be a playboy, and must be careful not to get into any scrapes, such as brawls and childish stunts.

The 'Ndrangheta is divided into higher and lower societies. The group of top-ranking bosses is known as *'Il Crimine'*, also called *'Provincia'*. Then there are the *locali*, confederations of different *'ndrine*, 'families' which include clans and blood relatives. These are the three levels, but it is between the higher and lower societies that the various ranks are articulated. There is the ritual that we have described, the oath that leads a *contrasto onorato* or non-associate to become an honourable young soldier, a *picciotto d'onore*. Then there are the *camorrista* and the *sgarrista*, lower ranks in the organization. Often those who are part of this hierarchy don't even know the names of the ranks: *santista*, *vangelo*, *trequartino*, *quartino*, *padrino*, *crociata*, *stella*, *bartolo*, *mammasantissima*, *infinito* and *conte Ugolino*. The last levels have just been discovered and it is interesting that they were not created in Polsi in Aspromonte, but in Milan.

What has always struck me about the bosses of the criminal organizations is their absolute spirit of sacrifice. It seems impossible, but how does a man hold out for decades against the 41-bis system, the state's 'hard prison regime': being cut off entirely from all family friends and associates while in prison? You understand it when you see how they live when they are out free or hiding as a fugitive, forced to stay locked up in their bunkers. Being a mafioso means fabricating a life of unhappiness. If you are an associate you know that you will end up dead or in jail. This is the price you pay when you want true power, the kind that enables you to decide the life and death of everyone else. That's why, before you build the house where you are going to live, you have to build a bunker, because you know that you can only live your life outside prison if you know how to go into hiding. Bunkers are a sign of misery and deprivation that is almost manifested architecturally, misery born of sacrifice and the self-perception of power.

Italy is the country that has the most bunkers in the world. In South America, drug traffickers hide in Amazonia, in what can be considered natural bunkers. In Italy, however, they are constructed, and people in Calabria and Caserta build the best bunkers in the world. Over and above being a hideout, the bunker is a philosophy of life, a concept that follows the logic of living in a constrained space, of never going out, of never seeing the light of day. Bunkers may be only as big as 100 square feet, the area of the inside of a car. They are minuscule lairs, impossible to find, where you live and command banks you will never enter, buy watches you will never wear, acquire cars you will never drive, while seeing your children once a year. And you'll fill those lairs with things that in some way reflect you: religious images, porn magazines, cars and watches, demonstrating that the mafia's power is more internal than external and doesn't exist to be flaunted.

There are areas, like Locride in Calabria, where the bunker is part of everyday life for everyone. It is built with thoughts of the future; maybe it won't be needed, but better to have one on the off chance. A bunker is already included in plans for a new home, as if provident parents were thinking about their children's future by preparing a worry-free refuge. It can always come in handy for a relative, a brother-in-law ... These hideaways are hard to find because, since most property is not registered at the Land Office, there is no complete toponymy of the region. So there are no maps, and the carabinieri (who have formed an ad hoc division to hunt them down) must rely on memory and their detailed knowledge of the territory.

There is a bunker in Platì which belonged to the Trimboli-Marando 'ndrina, built inside a wood-fired pizza oven. I've been there, I was brought there by the carabinieri of Colonel Valerio Giardina, who is at the forefront of the battle against the

'Ndrangheta in Locride. You climb into the oven and then, moving aside a block that slides on rails, you enter a tunnel that ends in a room from which another tunnel, about two hundred yards long, leads out to the open countryside. All just a little over a mile from the centre of town, in a modest peasants' house that is now impounded. When it was discovered, this particular bunker was 'cold', meaning that there was no fugitive hiding inside.

Another time, again in Platì, I was surprised to see a group of houses built near a waterway that had been covered up by the 'Ndranghetisti (a little like certain canals in Milan or Bologna that flow underground as cars pass above them). They did this because they built interconnected bunkers under the houses that in turn were all connected with the underground river, through which they could find another way out. The houses are run-down, but you can clearly see the opening mechanism concealed beneath the stone stairs leading to the first floor. The two staircases slide into the wall, leaving a space. A passage opens up, leading to a room that then connects to another tunnel, which leads to two neighbouring houses. They are all connected. Two fugitives were captured in these bunkers, which were discovered in 2001.

An ingenious system of pulleys, counterweights and ropes enabled the opening of another bunker, where Saverio Trimboli was arrested on 13 February 2010; a fugitive since 1994, he was accused of international drug trafficking. By moving a heavy concrete block and some bricks, you entered a very large space (over 300 square feet), where catalogues featuring watches could still be found, along with thirty scanners, twenty portable radios, devices to detect bugs and ten thousand euros in cash.

It is extremely difficult to discover a bunker. The special division of the carabinieri uses numerous methods, such as dumping a bucket of water on the ground to check the gradient. Because it's useless to rap on the walls: the other side will never be hollow, the reinforced concrete slides on tracks.

There is a bunker that I will not forget. One day the carabinieri took me to the countryside, where there was nothing but a chicken coop, and asked me: 'Where do you think the bunker is?' I looked around and there was nothing. I said: 'Maybe underground.' 'No, not underground.' The carabinieri had kept the area under surveillance for months. They spotted the fugitive walking around and smoking a cigarette, something which he evidently could not do in his hideout. When they got there, the fugitive, Domenico Trimboli – a boss known as *'u Crozza*, 'the skull', accused of drug trafficking and mafia association – had vanished. After about ten failed attempts, the carabinieri were convinced that there had to be a trapdoor into which Trimboli disappeared. When they were about to give up for the umpteenth time, a marshal in the Hunter Squadron noticed that a section of the masonry dry-wall that separated the garden from the chicken coop was not as damp as the rest. Even though little plants had grown among the stones, there was no moss. It was the moving part of a dry-wall that allowed access to the safe place. When a man hides like that he is willing to give up his life, surrender his soul and forsake sunlight, just to cling to his power. There have been bosses who have lost their sight living down there, bosses who earned millions and millions of euros per day and lived like that, under a chicken coop.

I wouldn't want these stories to seem like distant tales out of the Middle Ages, stories about '*terroni*', 'southern peasants'. The fact is that the fate of all of Italy is decided in those bunkers. Because it is in the North that the criminal organizations, especially the 'Ndrangheta, conduct their business. Lombardy is the region with the highest rate of criminal investments in Europe. The economy which these organizations infiltrate is Lombardy's, the health services are Lombardy's, the politics is Lombardy's. In this sense, Milan is the capital of Italian criminal affairs. All you have to do is take a map of the city and highlight all the contracts and jobs that are 'subjects of interest' or infiltrated by criminal organizations, in this case by the 'Ndrangheta: Santa Giulia,

Navigli Euro Milano, the Milano–Bergamo high-speed railway, the Milan–Bergamo highway, the Central Train Station, the new courthouse, Portello, City Life, Porta Garibaldi, the Milan-Rho Fair, metro line 5, the former Ansaldo area, a depot of the Milan transport agency, the Corvetto area, the customs agency.

My friend Nicola Gratteri, a courageous magistrate, has been telling me these stories for some time. But a recent investigation, conducted by Milan prosecutor Ilda Boccassini and Reggio Calabria prosecutor Giuseppe Pignatone, has confirmed them, reconstructing, among other things, the attempts on the part of Milan's 'Ndrangheta to break away from the organization in Calabria.

In San Vittore Olona, in the province of Milan, we have Carmelo Novella, known as *compare* Nuzzo. He is the godfather of the 'Ndrangheta in Lombardy, a body that is suitably called '*la Lombardia*'. His résumé includes years spent in prison for mafia association, weapons and drugs. Nuzzo has a revolutionary plan: to make Lombardy's *locali* independent from Calabria (until then they had been a branch of the Calabrian mother organization) and, at the same time, make them 'dependent' on their regional boss, namely, Nuzzo himself. As Nuzzo sees it, he can now manage Lombardy on his own, since it is in Lombardy that the economic heart of the organization lies. To attract a following, he rewards some associates by granting them rank, and even goes so far as to create new *locali* without seeking permission from central command in Calabria, stepping over the then boss of Milan's *locale*, Cosimo Barranca. Nuzzo therefore breaks the rules. This of course does not please central command, which decides to settle the matter, as is done in these cases.

Nuzzo knows that something is up because the Calabrian bosses at the upper echelons of the *provincia* (the highest rank) travel up to Milan every two weeks, yet they steer clear of meeting him, they avoid *him*, the nominal boss of Lombardy. But, above all, at a certain point the daughter of a boss from Gioiosa

Jonica gets married. There is a big celebration and Nuzzo is not invited, whereas his enemies are. Weddings are actually a time when meetings take place, when decisions are made. Not being invited to the wedding is a clear signal, a sign that Nuzzo is about to be 'sacked'. From that time on he's a dead man walking. To the point that his number two man sleeps with the door bolted and a pistol under his pillow, and is guarded by a hit man.

And a month later, in fact, on the afternoon of 14 July, Carmelo Novella is sitting at a table in a café in San Vittore Olona with some friends, under the portico. It is 5.45 when two guys, unmasked and wearing motorcyclist's vests, enter the café. One of the two orders a *'cappuccino bianco'*, a white cappuccino. The *barista* will remember it because it's an odd request, even a little comical: maybe he meant to order what a Milanese would have called a *cappuccino chiaro*, with extra milk. Then the two guys walk up to Novella's table outside. They call his name: 'Carmelo!' Novella, who has just stood up to order something, finds himself facing his killers: they shoot him, four times, from less than two yards away. When he sees the gun barrel, Novella tries to ward off the first shot, shielding himself with his arm. The other bullets, 38-calibre lead bullets, finish him off. The killers then calmly step over the body and move off on foot, walking swiftly and disappearing around the corner.

Carmelo Novella's sin was arrogance. Intercepted in his car on the way to the funeral, a boss tells the mother: 'He wanted to reach for the stars, but you can't touch the stars.' Her reply: 'You reap what you sow.' As if it were perfectly normal: you did wrong, you're punished for it.

With Carmelo Novella dead, Calabria wants to regain control of Lombardy. A year later, at another wedding – this one between Elisa Pelle and Giuseppe Barbaro, each the offspring of a boss – Domenico Oppedisano is named *'capocrimine'*, that is, the person at the top of the organization who commands all the families. His first official speech is made on 1 September 2009, at the shrine in

Polsi. It's exactly midnight, and in the sanctuary of this little village in Aspromonte they are celebrating the Madonna of the Mountain. The TV cameras which the carabinieri have hidden in the garden opposite the church record a group gathered in a circle, in a corner. Among them is the new boss of bosses, who wants to make things clear: 'Positions can't be assigned whenever we want, only twice a year. [. . .] And we must all do it together. The *Crimine* must be formed by members of the *locale*. All together.'

Attorney Giuseppe Neri is called in to restore order to a situation that had been threatening autonomy. His charge is to consult the bosses of each *locale* in order to nominate a new boss, subject to everyone's approval: a *'mastro generale'* (overall boss). In actuality, it is clear from the wire-tapping interceptions that Neri and several Lombardy bosses are playing both sides; they have no intention of letting go of their hold: 'The essential thing is that we be the ones to maintain contacts with those guys down there. That's what I want, he can be in charge here, but we'll be the ones making the decisions. We'll pick any old fool and make him a boss, we'll decide, let him be in charge.'

It's planned as a summit, a dinner with all the *locali* of Lombardy, in Paderno Dugnano, a village in Milan's outskirts, nine miles north of Lombardy's capital. We're not in Locri, in Calabria. We're not in the South. We're just outside the ancient gates of Milan. A dinner is arranged for 31 October 2009, at the Falcone-Borsellino Social Club in Paderno. How ironic! Holding a meeting of 'Ndrangheta associates in a club which bears the name of two anti-mafia magistrates famously assassinated by the Mafia. Only two representatives from each *locale* are invited to the dinner, about thirty people in all. The evening's organizer, Vincenzo Mandalari (boss of the Bollate *locale*), sees to all the details: the meeting place for everyone is the parking lot of a multiplex cinema and from there the bosses are shuttled to the club by car in several trips. 'Leave your cars here,' Mandalari instructs them. 'Leave your cell phones turned off, leave them here in the car, and come with me.' He also provides the heavies stationed in front of the club, to stand guard. He is the first to arrive at the Falcone-Borsellino club that evening: he has the horseshoe arranged his way, and has the windows covered with posters so no one can nose around from outside.

By 8.30 all the bosses are seated at the u-shaped table. The centre seats are reserved for Pino Neri and Vincenzo Mandalari. Their supremacy is clear: when one of the bosses gets up to pour some wine for the guests, he pours theirs first. The door to the kitchen is closed because it's time for the bosses to 'have a word' and no one should overhear them.

Before starting dinner, Pino Neri gives an introductory speech introducing the candidate for the role of *'mastro generale'* of Lombardy, who will be responsible for overseeing relations with Calabria. Neri proposes Pasquale Zappia and the voting follows, with Mandalari himself administering the roll-call vote. Neri's speech is that of a consummate politician. On the one hand he stresses the respect that the central command has for Lombardy, and in fact every Lombard *locale* will maintain its own sovereignty. But the rules must be adhered to, and to assign new ranks they must await clearance from Calabria. 'From now on, you must abide by terms and regulations.' He goes on: 'We are all, each of us, equal and responsible to the "mother".' Less than half an hour later, all the guests rise to make a solemn toast in honour of the new *mastro generale*, Pasquale Zappia.

Among those arrested in Milan in the major investigation into the 'Ndrangheta, *Il Crimine*, is a senior health official from the region, Carlo Antonio Chiriaco, medical director of the local health authority in Pavia.

Chiriaco managed more than 780 million euros and was sentenced for extortion in the first and second degree. He had acted as intermediary between several 'Ndranghetista families and a businessman who refused to pay the extortion. During his interrogation he told the judges: 'I am morbidly fascinated by the urge to pretend I am a criminal. I say certain things to see what effect it has on others.'

What the Milanese told themselves for years is that the Mafia does not exist in Milan, that it's far, far away. Instead, the control of the area is beginning to look more and more like that in the South. In Cisliano, for example, 12 miles from Milan, during a routine check in front of the restaurant La Masseria, one of the Valle clan's men blocked a car of carabinieri who were patrolling the area. These are things that used to happen only in Casal di Principe, in Platì, in areas where the mafias regimentally control the area.

Then, too, just like in the South, the organizations seek the support of the parties in power. And in areas where the *Lega Nord* holds power, even from the League. As evidenced by the investigation conducted by prosecutors Boccassini and Pignatone, in 2009 Pino Neri and other bosses made contact with a regional councilman in Lombardy, a member of the League; though the investigations show that the bosses asked him to support the election of a political ally of theirs, he was not arrested later. Moreover, in a 1999 interview Gianfranco Miglio, one of the fathers of the League, stated:

> I am in favour of maintaining the Mafia and the 'Ndrangheta. The South should adopt a statute based on the character of the controlling body. [. . .] I do not want to reduce the South to the European model, it would be an absurdity. There is good patronage as well, which determines economic growth. All in all, we must start from the notion that a number of phenomena typical of the South need to be constitutionalized.

The *Lega Nord* has essentially always presented a repressive opposition to criminal organizations; it has always fought against the bosses' obligatory presence in the North. Handcuffs. Suppression. Agreed, but that's not enough. Because the strength of criminal organizations lies in money, including legal money that the mob craves and has collected for decades. And the mafias' legal money also drenches the North.

I repeat it often, but maybe it's worthwhile, because the strength of those who oppose criminal organizations, even abroad, represents the decent part of society. I feel it deep inside and I read it in the rulings, in the polls, and in the analyses of hundreds of journalists, I hear it in the words of those who are truly fighting the 'Ndrangheta in Lombardy. Certainly it's law enforcement, it's the judiciary. But above all it's the honest segment of Calabrian society. It's the Italians who stopped organized crime in the US, the Turks who put an end to the Turkish mafia in Germany. There is always a decent part. That's why using repression alone is a mistake. Every time there is a raid they tell us that the Mafia has been defeated, because fifty or five hundred people have been arrested.

Unfortunately, criminal organizations are at the forefront of this country's economy. For example, they control food distribution: twenty thousand locations, a billion in revenue each year generated by restaurants alone, which is a tiny fragment of their business. Obstruction efforts should also start from here.

The investigation of Boccassini and Pignatone led to an unprecedented round-up: 160 Lombard associates were identified (though the total number would be much higher: 500), 15 *'locali'* in Lombardy, including one in Milan's city centre and others in Bollate, Erba, Cologno and Brianza. But, above all, the investigation brought to light the new mindset of the 'Ndrangheta, whose conduct has undergone a kind of 'genetic mutation' over the last ten years. Morphing into an 'entrepreneurial mafia', it has changed its focus from traditional homicides, kidnappings and major drug trafficking, to forms of control of various economic sectors (such as the building trade, excavation at construction sites and granting loans to people in need) and infiltration of public institutions at the local level. While there are, therefore, criminals in the organization, alongside them there are Lombard associates who are often free from any problems with the law.

The clans in the North already planned to grab a good contract for the Expo. But how do they win the contracts? The technique is to offer the lowest bid. The company that submits the lowest price for completing the project wins. Large firms are successful at being awarded big contracts because they subcontract to Mafia companies, which are cheaper: they ask for less. They are parasitical with regard to the state and good value for the developer. The clans win because they are able to offer competitive prices. They win because they control the waste sector and drug trafficking. They win because they are able to launder money in one of the largest telephone companies in Europe. They win because they control distribution to supermarkets. So they win even before pointing the gun, even before making the South pay a steep price for money that will then be poured into banks up North and given to entrepreneurs in the North who sometimes don't even notice the stench. Even government initiatives – like the former Finance Minister Giulio Tremonti's 'tax shield', which allowed for the legalization of hidden assets without having to pay back taxes or face prosecution for related crimes such as accounting fraud, or the law restricting electronic surveillance, which fortunately was not approved, or the bill regarding short trials, also thankfully not approved – are all measures or proposals that are likely to facilitate crime.

When we talk about organized crime, we reach a rather sad conclusion: what can we do, faced by all this? In reality things are not all dark, and it's crucial to talk about it. There is an army of individuals who battle criminal organizations on a daily basis, not only with machine guns and the scales of justice, but by doing their jobs well. One of the things these organizations fear most is people acting: acting with dignity, not yielding, not asking for what's rightfully theirs as though asking for a favour. Every time we think of organized crime as a problem that doesn't concern us, every time we say 'let them kill one another', we are handing the Mafia a huge gift. Every time a news broadcast manipulates the facts, we are doing the clan a favour. But when you feel that you are acting because these stories are your stories, when you hear that a mayor has been killed because he was doing his job well, and you feel like that mayor was your mayor; when you feel that these stories concern you because they rob you of your happiness, your rights, because they force you to go begging for a job, deny you a year-end bonus, and make you pay an exorbitant price for a house because the organizations invest heavily in cement, monopolizing the entire real-estate market in a big city; when you feel all of this, then something is changing.

There is a very apt saying by Tolstoy: 'It is impossible to put out fire with fire, to dry up water with water, and to destroy evil with evil.' As long as each of us does no evil, we are making them step back, and we are perhaps dreaming of a different Italy.

3

The Amazing Ability of the South

I want to tell you a story about courage and also, I think, about happiness. The story of a man from the North who moved to the South. Of a man from Brescia, in Lombardy, who at fourteen began working in a steel factory.

It is the 1960s. Union battles are raging, and Giacomo Panizza develops an ardent interest in social issues. At age twenty-three, however, he decides to enter the seminary and become a priest. The bishop of his diocese calls upon him to work with individuals with disabilities, those who are differently abled. With the 'handicapped', as some would say. Don Giacomo learns that a community of disabled people in Calabria has asked Brescia for help. There are no support structures, they are often fired from their jobs, their families can't look after them, the local governments do not consider them to be whole men and women. It's a story like many others. Except that this young priest gets an idea: rather than moving these people up north, he himself will move to the South.

When he arrives, things aren't all that easy. Don Giacomo has a strong Brescian accent, he's lived in Brescia all his life, and spoke his dialect there. Calabria seems like another world, with different rhythms, a different language, another way of being in the world. In addition, his parish is spread out over eight villages and there are logistical problems. Nonetheless he carries on and forms an association called *Progetto Sud*, Project South: a project that seeks to build community, to bring together people with disabilities and people without disabilities, to discuss the issue of disability. And one that considers the mafias an obstacle to self-fulfilment, to meeting together, to solving problems together.

There is a point in this story that for me expresses a clear sense of the meaning of courage and what it means to act courageously. In 1996 a property in Lamezia Terme was impounded, in the Torcasio clan's neighbourhood. It is the boss's house. The seizure has enormous symbolic value, because it's as if to say: the estate you built with dirty money is returned to the community. The Torcasio family is one of two clans that have dominated the Lamezia area for years. The other is the Giampà. The war between the two begins on 29 September 2000, when Giovanni Torcasio, boss of the clan, is killed by the Giampà family. From there a series of homicides is triggered, each time involving one or the other faction, and resulting in more than twenty deaths in little more than two years. To put an end to this vendetta, the families come up with the idea of a marriage: that is, they try to arrange a marriage between a Torcasio woman and an associate of the Giampà family, Giovanni Cannizzaro. In reality, the marriage plan is a ruse: what Giovanni actually brings to his fiancée's house is an Easter basket filled with three kilograms of explosives connected to a remote detonator. Something goes wrong, the bomb does not go off, so the Cannizzaros decide to settle the matter personally: they take up a 7.65 calibre gun and begin shooting at the designated victims, killing Nino Torcasio and seriously wounding his brother Domenico.

This is how things were done in Lamezia in those years. Which is why, despite the fact that the house was seized, no one wants to go and live there. When the mayor decides to assign the residence to the police, they threaten to strike and say that the new space isn't needed. It's not true, and in fact they will later move to another facility. No one wants to go to that house for two reasons: the first is that it is a symbolic building, where Giovanni and Antonio Torcasio had always lived. The other is that six yards away there is another house, where the very same Torcasio family continues to live. The houses are close by, in fact, with entrances and exits designed in such a way as to allow for a quick escape from one building to another in case of a threat.

The year is 2002, it's been six years since the seizure. Dino Mazzorana, at the time interim mayor of Lamezia Terme appointed by the prefect (the City Council had been dissolved due to mafia infiltration), asks Don Giacomo if he would like to take possession of the house that no one wants. Don Giacomo agrees; it's what he's been waiting for. He has this community of individuals around him, with families who are unable to take them in, who've lost their jobs, who must rebuild their day-to-day lives, who need a place to live. He has people with dystrophy, people with motor impairment, people with cognitive problems. He says yes.

The keys are handed over to him. But as soon as he shows up, Antonio Torcasio (the brother of Giovanni who was killed a few years earlier), recently released from prison, approaches him and says: 'Either we live here or nobody lives here.' Because that's what the mafias do with their properties: when a house is seized, they scorch it, take everything out, from the parquet floors to the door handles. They want to leave it abandoned as a message to the citizens: you see what the government does? It leaves everything in a state of neglect; it seizes property, then doesn't take care of it. In fact, Don Giacomo says: 'Each time I went in, something was missing. From radiators to the electrical wiring. One day I saw a Jacuzzi in the bathroom, the next day it was gone.'

Don Giacomo is not easily intimidated, however, and goes to inspect the house to see how he can make it accommodating. A woman calls him 'a priest sent by the devil, not by God'. There are many changes that have to be made in the house: he must first of all have the architectural barriers knocked down, so he has to look for a construction company, for workers. But no contractor in Lamezia wants to go against the Torcasios who run the cement business. They tell him: 'Don Giacomo, for you, anything you want. But at the Torcasio place, no. We have families.' It will take a good seven years to finish the job!

One of the reasons the work is needed is because the entrance to the seized home is common to that of the house where the Torcasios still live: each time Don Giacomo goes there, he has to ring the doorbell of the Torcasios to get in. During one of these visits, he is again threatened by Antonio, who tells him: 'We'll blow everything up rather than let mongoloids live here!' Antonio Torcasio will be arrested for this threat, but then he plea-bargains and will be sentenced to eight months of house arrest to be served in the very home that is six yards away from the community. The ultimate insolence.

Don Giacomo is placed under protective care. The protection programme obliges him to follow precise rules: he can't stay in one place for too long, he can't go to certain places, he must change his route often, he cannot go to the barber. At first he doesn't understand. 'Why can't I?' he asks. They explain to him that the tendency is to 'eliminate' people when they come out of the barber's, to shoot them just at that moment, because the message is: he got all spruced up for the photo on his grave.

After the threats he often has a dream, which is always the same: he sees two men, guns in hand, chasing another man, who in the end can't run anymore and collapses. The pursuers reach him, shoot him and run away. Then Don Giacomo goes over and sees that the man lying dead on the ground is actually himself.

Despite the fact that none of this stops, he carries on. He goes to find out how to change the name on the gas and electricity accounts. But at the Municipality they tell him: you have to open brand-new accounts because there are none there. 'How can that be? There were kitchens, chandeliers, Jacuzzis.' 'Right, but the accounts weren't in anyone's name.' Who paid? As is often the case with the Mafia, the building was illegal and so were all the utilities. They'd even forced the electrician to install an internet connection.

Notwithstanding all the difficulties, threats and delays, the community is launched. In it, people with disabilities live and work. Here I truly came to understand what the term 'differently abled' means: that it's not a polite way to say 'handicapped', but denotes having skills that people without disabilities don't have. In that situation of forced proximity, for the first time the bosses find themselves up against a priest who tells them: 'Look, I won't ever come here armed, we're only concerned with our community.' The point is that they saw people in wheelchairs, people who were unarmed, who by their vulnerability powerfully and vehemently affirmed the desire for legitimacy. Until then, all the properties seized in Lamezia Terme had been left vacant. The Municipality had never been able to reassign them to anyone. The bosses could not accept the fact that people in wheelchairs could come and defeat them.

At a certain point, about a year ago, Don Giacomo's community becomes the victim of a sneaky, cowardly attack. One evening, in front of another Progetto Sud location, a rehabilitation centre, two disabled individuals who work in the community have the brakes on their cars tampered with: two vehicles equipped for transporting people with disabilities. They are parked at the top of a very steep road, with two hairpin turns, which comes out on a very busy street. Fortunately, the driver of one of the cars immediately notices that the brakes aren't responding and manages to pull the handbrake. The other car is mercifully stopped by a tree.

The potency of this story is that it demonstrates a truth. Living and working in these premises means sending the town of Lamezia Terme a message: if you can reclaim the house of a boss, maybe you can reclaim society. Don Giacomo's community has been the guinea pig: it has pioneered the way to utilizing other seized assets, and has left its mark. And Don Giacomo, a man from the North, has fully understood the resourcefulness of the South. It is not enough to come and simply do things right. You must come and change them. Change them with the talents you have, without looking elsewhere for them. Only in this way, if you are someone who is forced to live differently, will you create a different Italy.

I learned of this story a long time ago when Don Giacomo invited me to the community. I've seen how they live there, I've seen that what a person lacks becomes an added value there. There is no resignation, rather a desire to act. By bringing these people together, Don Giacomo has succeeded in doing what all the others had failed to do.

A disabled woman, Emma, who works in the community, told me:

> Over and above being disabled, I am a person with rights and duties. So in addition to rights, I felt I also had some responsibilities to the region, because it is an area that has a huge scourge, the 'Ndrangheta, and I'm not comfortable there, I feel constrained in such oppressive surroundings. I can accept my disability because it is a natural fact, but I can't accept suffering inflicted by man.

4

Waste and Contaminants: The Toxic Mountain

You have to imagine Mont Blanc, 15,780 feet, the highest mountain in Europe. Or K2, 28,251 feet, the second highest mountain in the world. Or better yet, the highest one of all, Mount Everest, 29,028 feet. Well, even Everest is nothing compared to what could be the highest mountain on earth: the sum total of all the illegal waste managed by criminal organizations. This waste would form a mountain 51,181 feet high, with a base of 7.4 acres.

It's complicated, but I would like to try to tell a never-ending story, the story about the waste in Naples. There are kids sixteen years old, born in Naples, who have never seen their city free of garbage. The emergency has gone on for sixteen years, to the point that even the word 'emergency' is no longer adequate. Because an emergency is a single incident, an exceptional moment. If it's repeated year after year it is no longer an emergency. In Naples, it has become the norm, almost a material given: in summer it's hot, in winter it's cold, every year there is a waste crisis.

Everywhere I go I'm asked the same question: how is it possible that the waste problem in Naples hasn't been solved? There are tons of images, tons of instances that pass before my eyes when I talk about this subject, images and instances that everyone in my region has seen and experienced. For example, air conditioners have suddenly begun appearing in all the houses in the Naples and Caserta area, in rural and provincial towns where they had never been used before, because the stench was so strong that it drifted into the houses in summer, forcing people to keep the windows closed. And I remember an incident in 2008, in Maddaloni, in the province of Caserta, when schools were closed, postal carriers folded their arms, and outdoor markets were cancelled. A schoolteacher from Boscotrecase told me that she leaves the house in the morning and drives to Naples, where she teaches, carrying with her the smell of garbage which has saturated the car seats and her clothes, causing the students to make fun of her.

So why are there tons of garbage bags on the streets of Naples, sometimes piled as high as the first floor of the buildings? How come it never happens in Genoa, Milan and Bologna, but in Naples it does? The answer actually exists and it is simple. The waste cycle in Campania is based on the unrestrained prevalence of landfills. Over time, however, these landfills fill up and the court sequesters them. They are closed because of capacity issues and other reasons: the leakage of leachate, the liquid created by rainwater seeping into the waste or by the waste's decomposition. And so at some point the trucks can no longer dump into the landfills and the garbage remains on the streets. This generates hellish effects such as bonfires, which are lit to try to decrease the volume of garbage. There is one district in the Neapolitan area, the Giugliano–Villaricca–Qualiano triangle, which is now called the 'land of fires'. You can often see dense black smoke billowing up along the roadsides. The procedure is well established: the most proficient at setting the fires are Romas, young immigrants. The clans give them fifty euros for every pile burned. They bind the waste with tapes from videocassettes, then toss on some alcohol and gasoline and move away. They set fire to the tape with a lighter, and the tape acts as a fuse. In a few seconds everything is burned: foundry by-products, glues and greasy fuel-oil deposits, which as they burn contaminate every inch of soil with dioxin.

The landfills are full for two major reasons. The first is that segregated garbage collection, which started late compared to other regions, doesn't work; waste sorting is only done in a few districts in Naples (with excellent results, however). There is therefore a huge volume of garbage, which is simply allowed to accumulate and which over the years makes it necessary to find more and more landfills. From Chiaiano to Terzigno almost 84 per cent of the garbage is unsorted and ends up in landfills, whereas by law only 35 per cent should go there.

We Neapolitans represent a paradox, among other things, because Naples itself was the first city in Italy to have invented segregated garbage collection. In Ferdinand II of Bourbon's 1832 Compilation of Laws and Decrees of the Kingdom of the Two Sicilies we read that residents were required to keep the streets in front of their homes clean, 'taking care to pile the garbage to the side of their homes, and to separate any shards of glass or crystal into a separate pile'. The punishment for those who did not comply with this law and did not separate their waste was severe, and could even lead to imprisonment.

The second reason the landfills are full is that an attempt was made to solve the problem with incinerators, which many experts consider extremely harmful. According to a European norm, waste that, when burned, produces energy should be incinerated. To achieve this result, however, the waste must undergo a very complex process. Early in the process there must be separate collections to exclude all trash to be recycled. Plants for the production of RDF, refuse-derived fuel, must eliminate moisture from the solid waste, shred the material, and compress it into so-called 'eco-bales'. Almost immediately, however, the eco-bales produced by plants in Campania were no more than 'bundles' in which waste was crammed as it arrived, 'as is' so to speak. Moreover, the energy-recovery incinerator in Acerra did not begin operation until eight years after eco-bales began to be produced, and it only works in fits and starts: designed to burn 2,000 tons of garbage, in September it was only able to burn a little over 500 tons.

Even the geography of Campania's interior has been modified by the eco-bales. Travelling through the area between Naples and Caserta you can see huge black and white pyramids. They tried to dispose of them in the North and abroad, but nobody wants them because they are not composed properly. It would take fifty-six years just to get rid of the eco-bales accumulated to date. These stacks of eco-bales also contain moisture, which over time has fermented. There's no way of knowing what is actually inside them: there could be hazardous gases. They would have to be opened, taken apart and reassembled.

What the political centre-right and centre-left tried to do was disastrous and sketchy. Many mistakes were committed, wrong decisions were made. From 1998 to 2008 around 780 million euros a year were spent in compensation, consulting fees and land rental – about 8 billion euros over ten years, practically a fiscal appropriation! Antonio Rastrelli, President of the Campania Region from 1995 to 1999, is guilty of having come up with an ill-conceived, half-baked plan for waste disposal, which provided for incineration plants only, without worrying about segregated collection. His successor, Antonio Bassolino, is politically responsible for having signed a call for bids that would never work, since it was staked on economic expediency rather than on the plant's technological guarantees, and for not having kept watch. But what's worse is that Bassolino signed the agreement between the Waste Management Task Force and Impregeco, a company founded in 2002 by an alliance between the Ce4 consortium (an entity that the public prosecutor of Naples theorizes is at the complete command of the Casalesi clan via the Orsi brothers) and two other consortia in the Naples area (the NA1 and Na3). Its goal was to form a united alternative to the FIBE consortium (a subsidiary of the Impregilo group), which had won the contract for waste disposal in Campania. According to prosecutors, this was a plan devised by Nicola Cosentino and the Casalesi, who by so doing thought to bring the entire waste-management cycle into their own hands. Bassolino defended himself by saying that he had no knowledge of it: 'My role and my numerous obligations did not allow me to have specific, technical knowledge of the events.'

In 2006, Guido Bertolaso was called upon to resolve the problem. Bertolaso proposed building a landfill in the World Wildlife Fund nature reserve in Serre and shortly afterwards resigned. Giovanni De Gennaro then arrived on the scene as a transitional commissioner. Strictly military in temperament, he carried out orders, bringing them to completion and opening as many landfills as possible: Terzigno, San Tammaro, Sant'Angelo Trimonte, Savignano Irpino, Macchia Soprano and even in Serre, in the WWF reserve. In 2008, Bertolaso returned. When it came to making decisions potentially dangerous to the health and welfare of the citizens and the region, he had always preferred to focus on the immediate results. The landfills of Villaricca and the heaps of eco-bales are a concrete, visual demonstration of his failure. All of them, with different responsibilities, have failed. No one has ever really dealt with the reclamation of the contaminated lands. And the irony of it is that organized crime has already set its sights on this issue. The people who helped pollute the land now intend to make more money by reclaiming it.

Those who have profited from this state of affairs are those in the business that has the highest earnings in Campania: the Camorra. There is no crisis in the ecomafia business. A fact to keep in mind: in 2009 alone, according to data from the environmental association, Legambiente, the ecomafias realized an illegal accumulation of resources worth over 20 billion euros, about a quarter of the Mafia's total proceeds. The ecomafia's earnings are equal to that of Telecom Italia, ten times that of Benetton.

There is a precise moment when this all began. In Villaricca, a town near Naples, a meeting took place in 1989 that included Camorristi from Pianura, contractors, masons, politically connected friends and landfill owners. It is the baptismal dinner of the ecomafia system. The Camorra declares that it is willing to provide land and pits to dispose of toxic waste. In exchange it is prepared to give up part of the money it receives from contractors and donate it to the politicians who will then allow unrestricted dumping, turning a blind eye. Campania is chosen because it is a primary crossroads for international waste routes to Africa. Passing through Naples, toxic waste is dumped in the Maghreb, in Liberia, in the Horn of Africa, in Somalia. So why not let it stay in Campania? You save a trip, you earn more.

In Campania every inch of land has its own specific consignment of waste. A farmer, while ploughing his land, might even find shredded liras, dumped illegally. Cemeteries are also known to do periodic exhumations, removing what younger gravediggers call the *arcimorti* (ultra-dead): those who have been dead for over forty years. They are supposed to dispose of the remains, along with all other cemetery material, through specialized enterprises, but the cost of disposal is extremely high. So the cemetery directors give the gravediggers a kickback to handle it by burying everything in the Caserta countryside. All you'd have to do is dig around with your hands or a kitchen spoon and you'd find skulls and ribcages. So many of them were dumped, as the Carabinieri health-protection services in Caserta discovered in February 2006, that now when people pass by they make the sign of the cross, as if it were a cemetery.

Roads are also built with toxic waste material. The expressway that connects the Palma Campania interchange with the towns of the Vallo di Lauro – a one-and-a-half-mile escape route in case of an eruption by Vesuvius – was impounded by Nola's carabinieri in March 2010: the spring rains had caused asbestos fibres to emerge from the asphalt. The 162 acre-feet of asphalt had been obtained by mixing crushed asbestos, hazardous special waste and compost from Anthony Iovino's dump.

In 2008, in Crotone in Calabria, a police operation called Black

Mountains revealed the presence of arsenic, zinc, lead, indium, germanium and mercury originating from an industrial plant. Instead of being disposed of in a landfill, these substances were used in construction: 350,000 tons of toxic materials were used to build public housing, private homes, a harbour dock, roads and, worst of all, three schoolyards in Crotone and Cutro. Medical tests performed on 290 students from various schools detected high serum concentrations of zinc, cadmium, nickel, arsenic, uranium and lead.

For ecomafias, finding land and pits where they can dump and hide stuff is always critical. When digging to construct buildings, foundations become ideal places in which to conceal garbage. For the Camorra anything that's empty becomes a space to fill.

Often, eco-bales are stored on the lands of farmworkers and small growers. The Camorra buys the acreage from the farmers at expedient rates, far below market price, then rents it to the state for millions of euros a year. There are actual intermediaries who handle the purchase and selling of these lands: as soon as they know where the eco-bales should be stored, the intermediaries go to the landowners and buy the tract at bargain prices, especially when dealing with people who need money immediately, like farmers afflicted with cancer or burdened with debt, or families with children to marry off.

I have always wondered how a farmer can sell his land to have toxins dumped there. I'm from the South and, as every southerner knows, the cultivation of fruit is sacred in the South, it's one of our strengths. We have always exported lemons, apples, pears, peaches and almonds throughout the world. So how is it possible that the growers themselves and the landowners have betrayed us like that, by selling some of their land to have it become a receptacle for poisons? The truth is that they were duped. In the 1980s and 1990s the big supermarket chains forced them to keep the price of fruits and vegetables down, threatening that otherwise they would go to Spain or Greece to buy them.

Unable to cope with the competition, growers were forced to sell a portion of their land to the clans, who began using it for illegal waste dumping. With that money the farmers were able to continue growing peaches, pears, lemons and annurca apples: they could continue doing their job. But that path resulted in calamity: they sold out, and the government left them on their own.

Gradually, even the Camorra had to face the problem of these toxins. A story that informant Gianfranco Mancaniello tells is interesting: he describes a meeting with a boss who had received a proposal from contractors in the north-east, wanting him to take care of several tons of toxic waste. So the boss begins to think about how many landfills he'll need and under which ground he can dispose of the poisons. An associate reminds him: 'But we'll contaminate the groundwater by doing that.' And the boss replies, 'What the fuck do we care, we'll drink mineral water.' Criminal organizations are ready to turn anything and everything into a business. Profit, profit, profit: those are the three cardinal rules of the organizations. In other words: if we don't do it, others will, and if others do it they will become stronger than us and we'll cease to exist. As a result of this logic, southern Italy – the Naples and Caserta region in particular – has been drowned in toxic waste, which has poisoned the countryside and the streets.

We must never forget, however, that the North's toxic waste is also dumped in the South. In the early 1990s Campania had the greatest number of legal landfills in operation. They could have been adequate for decades and decades, but because they were illegally filled with waste from the North, they became saturated prematurely. From that point on, the system broke down. That's why Naples' garbage is everyone's garbage. Let's remember that, every time the North refuses to help the South as if it were a problem that doesn't concern them, every time the politicians of the North refuse to accept waste from Naples. In reality the country is all interconnected, like a system of communicating vessels. Revealing the disposal of the North's toxic waste in the

Giugliano area, informant Gaetano Vassallo stated: 'The liquid wastes were so contaminated that all the rats immediately died when the wastes were dumped.'

Campania has become the dumping ground for many northern Italian companies, because the line item for the disposal of 'special waste', as opposed to household waste, is a big expenditure in a company's budget. Relying on an intermediary who has contacts with the clan results in greatly lowering this cost. The market price for the proper disposal of toxic waste involves costs ranging from 21 to 62 euro cents per kilo, excluding transport. The clans provide the same service at 9 or 10 euro cents per kilo, including transport. An 80 per cent savings over market prices.

How do they manage to dispose of this toxic waste, when these materials are duly classified by the European Waste Catalogue? The mechanism is simple, it's called *giro di bolla*, and it is the mechanism whereby truckloads of toxic waste, which would otherwise have a high cost of disposal, are magically transformed into innocuous garbage that can be sent to a landfill without any problem. Each load of waste is accompanied by a bill of parcel, *bolla*, which indicates the hazardous degree of the substance. Companies that want to save money turn to an intermediary who transports the toxic waste to a warehousing centre. There the bill of parcel is easily modified with the stroke of a pen. Alternatively the toxic waste is often mixed with ordinary waste, so as to dilute the toxic concentration and lower the hazard level in the document as well.

One of the most incredible outcomes is that organizations sometimes not only manage to hide the toxic waste, but actually turn it into fertilizer that can be sold! And so the clans even go so far as to make money from selling poisons, as shown by Operation Fly, one of numerous investigations into the illegal trafficking of waste along the north–south corridor. I've tried to list several of them here:

- Cassiopeia (2003): Every week, from North to South, 40 semis loaded with waste-dumped cadmium, zinc, lead paint discards, sludge from wastewater purification plants, assorted plastics, arsenic, steelworks scraps and lead.
- Mother Earth (2006): Coordinated by the Santa Maria Capua Vetere's Public Prosecutor's Office. Printer toner from offices in Tuscany and Lombardy were dumped at night between Villa Literno, Castelvolturno and San Tammaro by trucks officially carrying compost. The lands were saturated with hexavalent chromium, a chemical element that, when inhaled, lodges in the red blood cells and in the hair, causing ulcers, respiratory and kidney problems, and lung cancer.
- Fly (2004): In Umbria and Molise 120 tons of special waste from metallurgical industries and hospitals in northern Italy were illegally dumped. Four acres of land near the coast of Molise were cultivated with fertilizer derived from this waste. The grain produced contained a very high concentration of chromium.
- King Midas (2003): An investigation by Naples' public prosecutor into over 40,000 tons of waste from central and northern Italy dumped into abandoned quarries and farmlands in the province of Naples.
- Adelphi (1993): In one of the earliest operations, the Naples Anti-Mafia Directorate investigated the transport of toxic waste from Veneto, Lombardy and Piedmont to Campania, in Pianura.
- Greenland (2002): The prosecutor of Spoleto investigated the discovery of toxic waste in six farms in Umbria, Lazio, Tuscany and Puglia.
- Murgia Violata (2002): The Prosecutor's Office in Bari investigated the transport of toxic waste from Tuscany, Lazio, Lombardy, Veneto and Liguria, dumped in the farmlands of the Province of Bari.

- Econox (2002): The Cosenza Prosecutor's Office investigated the transport of toxic waste from Calabria, Lazio and Campania to Cosenza.
- Eldorado (2003): Illegal trafficking of hazardous waste, shipped to Lombardy from the South to be 'mixed' with masses of garbage from the streets of Milan and other materials, so as to then pass as non-hazardous waste and be dumped in a landfill in Puglia.
- Dirty Pack (2007): An investigation by the Prosecutor's Office in Naples that brought to light illicit trafficking in toxic and hazardous waste products from Campania, shipped to steel-manufacturing companies operating in Udine and Brescia.

Everyone profits from the waste-management business. Criminal organizations profit. Politicians profit. Collection companies profit: those in Campania are among the most powerful in Italy, capable of forging relationships with the biggest groups in the world. The consortia profit: groups of several municipalities that join together to obtain cheaper prices for segregated collection, though then becoming fertile ground for patronage, rigged contracts and inflated invoices. A sphere where politics, clans and business concerns meet.

An inquiry conducted by Naples public prosecutors Alessandro Milita and Giuseppe Narducci has shown that these consortia have become the real centre of power in criminal organizations. Central to the investigation is the relationship between former Undersecretary of State for Finance Nicola Cosentino and waste-sector dealings conducted by brothers Sergio and Michele Orsi (the latter murdered by the terrorist arm of the Casalesi clan in June 2008, shortly after he began giving statements to the magistrates). The Orsi brothers' businesses, such as the public–private partnership Eco4, are considered by the investigating magistrate to be 'genetically linked to and operational with the Casalese Camorra'.

According to informant Gaetano Vassallo, Cosentino exercised absolute control of 'hiring, appointments and jobs'. To the point of claiming: 'I am Eco4.' As Michele Orsi said, 70 per cent of the hiring in the company was 'done to coincide with elections'.

Anything and everything has been dumped in the landfills and in the Campania countryside. In Giugliano della Campania, in Schiavi and in Tre Ponti: 590,000 tons of sludge and sewage containing asbestos, sediments containing trichloroethylene; and 600,000 tons of automotive tyres and industrial equipment come from various centres each year.

In the Pianura landfill, between 1988 and 1991, the following waste arrived from Acna Cengio (in Savona province), known for dye manufacturing: 1 billion 300 million cubic metres of sludge; 300,000 cubic metres of sodium; 250,000 tons of poisonous sludge containing cyanide; 3.5 million cubic metres of toxic tars containing dioxins, amines, organic compounds derived from ammonia and containing nitrogen.

In the rural areas of Acerra, between 1995 and 2004: 1 million tons of industrial sludge from Porto Marghera, in the comune of Venice; 300,000 tons of chlorinated solvents.

In the districts of Bacoli, Giugliano and Qualiano: 1.8 tons of 'non-hazardous' waste; 190,000 tons of partially radioactive waste from hospitals; 2 million tons of material resulting from demolition and reconstruction.

Agriculture in these places, which used to export fruit and vegetables to as far as Scandinavia, has fallen sharply. The fields wither and lose their fertility, and the fruit that does grow is sickly. Moreover, people are constantly dying of cancer. The figures are striking. According to a 2008 survey conducted in the province of Naples and Caserta by the ISS, the national institute of health, there has been an increase in mortality from lung, liver, stomach, kidney and bladder cancer, as well as congenital malformations. These cases are mainly concentrated in an area that straddles the two provinces, where sites for the illegal disposal of toxic waste are more numerous. Even the World Health Organization talks about a staggering surge in cancer incidences in this area: the percentage is 12 per cent higher than the national average. In many parts of the region, cancer is not the unfortunate outcome of bad luck, but the consequence of deliberate actions on the part of criminal entrepreneurs: actions that all too many have an interest in perpetrating. The illnesses linked to the presence of toxic waste are a silent plague that no one talks about, difficult to monitor partly because those who are able to often go to seek treatment in the North.

Yet how many times have we been told that the 'emergency' is over? How many times have they told us 'We've resolved it'? Seven times in just two years Silvio Berlusconi declared that the crisis had been resolved:

1 July 2008: 'By the end of July, the city of Naples and the municipalities in the Neapolitan province will be cleaned up.'

18 July 2008: 'The emergency has passed, we have disposed of fifty thousand tons of waste, Naples and Campania will go back to being like other Western cities, orderly and clean.'

26 March 2009: 'Today is a historic day for Campania, with the inauguration of the energy recovery incinerator in Acerra we have definitively overcome the crisis.'

30 September 2010: 'The government has totally resolved the problem of waste.'

22 October 2010: 'Within ten days the situation in Terzigno will be back to normal.'

28 October 2010: 'In three days there will be no more garbage in Naples.'

2 November 2010: 'We made a commitment, we resolved it all in a few days.'

Though the last statement was made on 2 November, in December there were still 3,000 tons of garbage in Naples and 8,000 tons throughout the province. When you hear 'Terzigno', when you see people blocking the trucks and you wonder why they are protesting, why they are making such a racket, remember that their desperation is generated by the fear of being poisoned.

For the government, the solution for getting the garbage off the streets is always the landfill: open another landfill, a second one in Vesuvius National Park. At one time it had been a beautiful place, where the Roman emperors spent their summer holidays. Now it's covered with trash. The residents of Terzigno will no longer stand for the so-called solution to getting the garbage off the streets: namely, dumping it in the landfill, with no controls, as has been done up till now, further contaminating the land. Their land has already been contaminated. That's why they don't trust the promises, that's why they make such a racket. Sixteen years of 'emergency' can demoralize and destroy the soul of an entire people. Sixteen years of the garbage crisis have driven out Naples' capital, have led Neapolitans to be identified with garbage and even caused them to lose all hope of seeing their city change.

It reminds me of a piece by Eduardo De Filippo, from his TV series called *Peppino Girella*, set in a poor household in Naples:

'Andrea, what can you do? It's nothing serious.'

'This too is nothing, right? It's always nothing. It's always nothing serious, that's how we've resolved every situation: it's nothing. We have no food, it's nothing; we're in need, it's nothing; the boss dies and I lose my job, so what, it's nothing; they deny us the right to live, it's nothing; they take away our air, what can you do? It's nothing serious. It's always nothing . . . How beautiful you are, how beautiful you were, and look at what I've become. By always saying "it's nothing", we've become two nothings, you and I.'

These words are seared into our consciousness, especially if we are Neapolitan. They deny us the right to live, they take away our air: 'It's nothing.' It's that way every time we stand for it, every time we believe the promises and welcome the politicians as liberators. Yet by standing for it, by considering it all normal, by saying 'it's nothing' to everything, we risk becoming 'nothings' ourselves.

5.

The Earthquake in L'Aquila

In July 1883 the philosopher Benedetto Croce was vacationing with his family in Casamicciola, Ischia. A boy of seventeen at the time, he was getting ready to have supper with his mother, father and sister, and was about to take his place at the table. All of a sudden he saw his father sway, as if weightless, and immediately drop to the floor, while his sister shot up to the ceiling. Terrified, he looked around for his mother and joined her on the balcony, from which they fell together. He lost consciousness and was buried up to his neck in the rubble. For many hours his father spoke to him, before passing away. He told him: 'Offer a hundred thousand liras to whoever saves you.' Benedetto would be the sole survivor of his family killed by the earthquake.

The annals of earthquakes are part of Italy's history. There is no family that does not recall experiencing one directly or indirectly. I have my mother's stories about the Irpinia earthquake of 1980. I was one year old, and my mother often recalls the nights spent in the car, feeding me nothing but mashed fruit. For Italians, earthquakes are not an unfamiliar occurrence. Yet, whenever there is one, it always seems to be the first, it seems like the first time we're experiencing such a tragedy. Each time we have the feeling that we are unprepared, or so it seems, given what happened in L'Aquila.

Since the 1990s, L'Aquila had successfully accomplished a miracle: it had become a university town. Like Urbino and other towns in central Italy, it had managed to become a veritable citadel of learning. These towns are the Italian version of American

44

college campuses, or, better yet, they are more attractive than college campuses because they are places that already seem naturally predisposed to becoming communities. Young blood flows into these towns and radically transforms them: the evenings stretch out, the streets are more crowded, rents increase, life begins to adapt to the typical rhythms of a youthful district, full of students from different parts of Italy and from abroad.

In L'Aquila there is a building that is very well known: the Casa dello Studente, students' residence. One hundred and twenty students from out of town live there, in fifty rooms. Dating from the mid-1960s, the building is seven stories high. It is a dormitory that is lived in all day, complete with dining hall, computer room, administrative offices. To live there you have to win a scholarship, then do well in your exams, uphold a high average – in short, you have to earn a bed in the residence at Via XX Settembre 46.

Marco lives in the Casa dello Studente, in room 208. Twenty-one years old, from Sora, in the province of Frosinone, he is in L'Aquila to study psychology. He is in his third year, not much longer to go till graduation. Until the year before he'd lived in the residence run by the Salesians, but Marco is a good student, has good grades, and was able to get a scholarship and lodging at the Casa dello Studente on Via XX Settembre.

Luciana lives in the same building on the third floor, room 308. Nineteen years old, from San Giovanni Rotondo, she is in L'Aquila to study medicine because she has a dream: to wear the white coat. The same dream shared by Michelone, room 407/S, whose name is actually Hussein Hamade. Michelone is an Arab-Israeli boy, who has also come here to study medicine. Michelone has very clear ideas about his future: after graduation, he wants to specialize in the United States, but before going to America, he wants to marry Chezia, an Italian girl he's met in L'Aquila, who lives a few floors down in the Casa dello Studente.

Angela also fell in love in L'Aquila. She is twenty-two, from

45

San Nicandro Garganico in Puglia. She moved here to study engineering, found housing in room 312 and met Francesco, a boy from L'Aquila who is the night guard in the building.

Luca, on the other hand, had to leave his girlfriend behind to come to L'Aquila. He left Giada in Rieti, his home city. They met in high school and from their love a baby girl, Marta, was born who is now seven months old. It was not an easy choice to decide to have a child while still studying, but they did it, without giving up their dreams. She wants to be a musician and studies at the Conservatory; he wants to become a computer engineer and that's the reason he came here to study. He rooms with Marco, the boy from Sora, in room 208 on the second floor.

Alessio has a girlfriend, Marianna, at the Casa dello Studente. They don't live on the same floor but are able to see each other from the windows. It's to be close to her that a few months ago he moved from the private apartment where he was living to the students' residence, room 412/A. He too won a scholarship and has only four more exams to take to complete his degree with a major in Computer Science. He has so many plans: after graduation he would like to spend some time abroad and learn a new language. He studies a lot but he's a fun guy who likes to play basketball.

Davide instead plays volleyball as a defensive specialist on the Vasto Magica Team. He's from Vasto, in the province of Chieti, and came to L'Aquila to study Engineering Management. He's in his first year but has already taken three exams. He did well on all of them and he's very pleased. Right after Easter he must take the most difficult exam of all: Calculus 2. He has to take it, to keep up, because otherwise he's in danger of losing the scholarship that enables him to live at the Casa dello Studente, in room 411/B. Davide always has a smile on his face, even if he does not have an easy life: he recently lost his father to an illness and has become the one the entire family relies on.

On the night between 5 and 6 April 2009 there are not many

students at the Casa dello Studente, only about thirty. Over the weekend many students returned home: with just a few more days till Easter, some decided to start their vacation a few days early and return immediately afterwards. Others are still not back at the Casa because they are unnerved by the continuous tremors that have been making the city tremble for more than four months. They are frightened because they do not feel safe in that building. They heard it creaking after each tremor and cracks had appeared in the walls, growing bigger and bigger. Many students, fearing an earthquake, decided to brave the cold and sleep outdoors: they even organized a kind of *notte bianca*, an all-nighter, for the tenants of the Casa dello Studente. Michelone is also invited, but he doesn't go because the exam is coming up in a few days. And besides, being Arab-Israeli, he's used to devastations and makes light of his friends' fear of an earthquake: 'Guys, after putting up with the kamikazes in Gaza, do you think I came here to die in the middle of this bucolic paradise?' His family had helped him move from a troubled land so he could have a better future.

And so the only ones left in the Casa dello Studente are those who still have classes to attend or exams to prepare for. Marco, the psychology student, arrives at ten o'clock at night after a weekend spent with his family in Sora. Before going to bed he calls his mother to tell her that everything is okay and that he will keep his mobile phone turned on during the night, so they can be in touch in case of any tremors. They are all students from out of town, many of them aren't used to earthquakes. Angela, the girl from Puglia, is scared, so she asks Francesco, her boyfriend from L'Aquila, to spend the night with her. Francesco isn't on duty as a security guard that night; he sleeps there just to reassure her.

Nobody wants to sleep alone that night. Luciana and Antonella ask Davide to come down to the third floor so all three of them can sleep in the same room: in case of an earthquake, they can all run out together. The first shock occurs at 10.44 p.m.: Davide's mother calls him from Vasto to tell him to get out of the building, but he's tired and wants to sleep so he can be in good shape to hit the books the next day. Besides, it's cold outside. Alessio and his girlfriend, Marianna, frightened, decide instead to leave and go to Marianna's sister, who also lives in L'Aquila and has a house with a yard, allowing for an easy escape in case of danger. Marianna's sister invites them to spend the night there, but Alessio has to get up early the next morning for a class. And he doesn't feel safe at Marianna's sister's house. He'd rather go back to his room at the Casa dello Studente. So he leaves Marianna at her sister's place and goes back to Via XX Settembre. It is now 1.30 a.m., 6 April. Ezio, his roommate, is still awake. The tremors keep them from sleeping. Alessio and Ezio start talking to allay their fear; they decide to sleep in their clothes, with their shoes on, to be ready to flee. The stairs are close to their room: if they feel the building start to shake they can reach the stairs quickly and get out.

At 3.32 a.m. the most powerful shock is felt: measuring 5.8 on the Richter scale, it causes the north wing of the Casa dello Studente to collapse. The final tally of the earthquake will list 308 victims, including 53 university students and 20 children, 1,500 persons injured, more than 65,000 displaced, and 23,000 houses destroyed in the five provinces of Teramo, Pescara, Chieti, Ascoli Piceno and L'Aquila. At the Casa dello Studente the phones begin ringing: many of them ring and ring, unanswered, like that of Davide. The room on the third floor, where he was sleeping with Luciana and Antonella, gave way in a kind of domino effect onto the second floor, then the first, then the ground floor, before plummeting into the dining hall, in the basement. Only Antonella miraculously manages to get to safety. Luciana and Davide don't make it.

Alessio's phone does not ring, however. His father Roberto, from Penne, in the province of Pescara, also feels the quake and begins calling him, but maybe the lines are congested. Then he turns on the television and sees that L'Aquila is the epicentre. He sees that at the Casa dello Studente firefighters are helping the kids make their way out. Alessio is a young man who always keeps him informed, he never lets his parents worry. The father begins to lose hope. He calls a friend of Alessio who tells him: 'I'm trying all the phones, Alessio is the only one who isn't answering.' Roberto tries calling everyone in L'Aquila: carabinieri, firefighters, the police. No one answers, or, if they do, they tell him to leave the line free for emergencies. Then at 4.30 a.m. he manages to find out from Alessio's girlfriend Marianna, who had spent the night at her sister's house, that Alessio is trapped in the rubble; they can hear Ezio, his roommate, screaming, however, so they must both be alive. 'When you hear them say he's trapped, you picture barred doors and windows maybe, but instead they were trapped under there with an entire building on top of them, and couldn't get out.' Roberto sets out from Penne with his other sons to go to L'Aquila. It's dawn and they find everything cordoned off. When he gets to the Casa dello Studente, Roberto finds Marianna who again tells him: 'Don't worry! We can hear Ezio!' At 10.30 a.m. the firefighters pull Ezio out, alive. Alessio's father is joyous, it rekindles his hope that his son will be alive as well. After all, the two boys slept in the same room, separated only by a nightstand: if Ezio is still alive, Alessio must also be alive. The firefighters continue to dig and a little at a time bring him objects belonging to Alessio: his laptop case, then an envelope full of notes wishing him luck on his degree, the shoulder bag he was never without. At one point his father asks the fireman: 'What about my son, when will you bring him out to me?' At 3.30 p.m. the firefighter returns with Alessio's wallet: 'He hugged me and I understood.'

Alessio's body was the first to be pulled from the rubble. After that they continued digging and hoping. The search was long and difficult, partly because a floor plan of the Casa dello Studente could not be found. Gabriele, one of the tenants who was able to get out safely, guided the firefighters as they tried to find his friends. He was the one who showed them where the rooms were, told them who was inside. It took three days to recover the bodies of the eight students who didn't make it. Marco, Luciana, Michelone, Angela, Francesco, Luca, Davide and Alessio lost their lives under the rubble on the night of 6 April.

Victims of the earthquake, or so they were described. But perhaps that's not accurate. According to the report of the experts appointed by L'Aquila's public prosecutor, the collapse of the north wing of the Casa dello Studente was due not only to the earthquake but also to a series of flaws and attempts to cut corners during the design and implementation phase of the construction and subsequent improvements. The experts' findings indicate that the collapsed wing was lacking a support column, unlike the other two wings which in fact held up: a support that was deliberately omitted from the plan. This omission led to a weakness in that part of the structure. The presence of the column would have been crucial in preventing the collapse. The lack of the pillar – the report reads – is one of the contributing factors leading to the collapse of that section of the building.

Of course, this is the judgement and these are the findings of one of the parties to the court proceedings, considerations that will have to be confirmed or not in the course of a criminal trial which will see eleven people charged. Nevertheless the report points out the following irregularities in the building's construction:

1. Studies were never carried out to determine the suitability of the building to the intended change of purpose and use. It was a building zoned for shops, offices and residential occupancy.
2. The building had been maintained in a state of poor repair with regard to its structural elements.
3. The reinforcements at the base of the pillars were in very bad condition.
4. The concrete used was of inferior quality.

5. The structural design of the building was marked by serious flaws in planning and calculation.
6. In a highly seismic area, the force of seismic activity was not taken into account.
7. An additional basement level was put in beyond the one called for in the plan.
8. Work was carried out that was inconsistent with the permits issued.

It seems incredible, yet the students had noticed for some time that there was something wrong with that building. They didn't feel it was safe and they could tell by the continuous tremors that the situation was worsening. The cracks were getting bigger and bigger, a nail could be pressed into the wall simply by pushing with your thumb. Not only that: there was a decaying column in the dining hall, 'rotted away' some students say, which in fact had been cordoned off, the tables moved as far away as possible.

The succession of earthquakes had begun in mid-December of 2008 with a slight tremor, but from January the shocks intensified. Within a few months four hundred of them had been recorded. On their own the students had then begun doing some research about L'Aquila's earthquakes and the area. Some had even started recording the tremors and their magnitude day by day. And when a student consulted the dorm's custodian to find out whether the building was up to standard, to see a document certifying that it was earthquake-resistant, she was reassured. The building can withstand an earthquake, they tell her, not to worry: 'L'Aquila trembles but it does not collapse! [. . .] Before this building collapses, all of L'Aquila must collapse. This is the safest area of the city.' In the report of the prosecutor's experts we read instead that not only had the residence been built without taking into account the potential force of seismic activity, but it was partially built 'with shoddy concrete'. That is, to skimp on costs a lot of water had been used, skimping on safety.

When on 30 March, a week before the tragedy, a tremor that was stronger than the others was felt, the students had asked the company that owns the property to send a building inspector to do an on-site check. They wanted to know whether staying in the building was dangerous, whether they should move. The manager of the inspection office comes to examine the building but does not report anything in particular. Everything is fine, he says. Following that inspection the students' representative goes to the architect and says: 'I didn't come all the way from Calabria to die here.' But the architect again reassures her. If they're really afraid, he advises them to sleep in the study hall with their clothes and shoes on. The same study hall that later collapsed.

The fact that the Casa dello Studente was not a safe structure was not just an idea of the students who watched the cracks widen and the columns rot away. It had also been put in writing. In 2006 the firm Collabora Engineering, which later became Abruzzo Engineering, had conducted a study on the buildings in the Abruzzo region at the request of the Regional Government and the Civil Protection agency; the Casa dello Studente on Via XX Settembre had been included among the 135 buildings categorized as having 'critical structural issues'. It would have cost 1,470,000 euros to structurally modify the student residence to comply with standards, a ton of money to make all 135 buildings safe. Nevertheless, the students' complaints went unheard, and their fears were met repeatedly with reassurances.

Even the National Major Risks Commission, which convenes in L'Aquila on 31 March, six days before the earthquake, prefers not to create alarm. Present at the meeting are members of Civil Protection, volcanologists and physicists, and all in all to them the situation appears normal.

In the face of such facts you begin to realize how critical it is to do things properly, how important it is to comply with the rules. Only with the devastation caused by the tragedy do you really understand that if the rules had been complied with, if the people who constructed the building had been given the opportunity to do things correctly, perhaps that building might not have become a grave for so many young people. Only when tragedy strikes, a catastrophe, do we really understand that the rules are by no means intended to constrain business, to create hurdles for companies, but rather they are a way of protecting life, of creating peace of mind, of affording everyone the chance to live without worry. The story of the Casa dello Studente, on the other hand, is symbolic of the criminal conduct, widespread in our country, of those who have built parts of the city with substandard concrete, saving on the cost of building materials, without regard for the fact that people made of flesh and blood would go to live in those 'time bombs'.

On 6 April 2009 entire buildings, even newer ones, collapsed in just a few seconds: they literally crumbled. Entire buildings reduced to a pile of rubble due to an earthquake of medium intensity, which elsewhere would probably not have caused the same ruin. Suffice it to say that the Nuova Casa dello Studente, the new student housing in a Jesuit building dating back to the seventeenth century, and therefore certainly not built according to modern seismic criteria, remained standing. The Casa dello Studente on Via XX Settembre was built in the 1960s, in the twentieth century!

Investigations carried out by the Prosecutor's Office in L'Aquila into the tragic collapses involve around two hundred buildings. Among them is San Salvatore Hospital, inaugurated in 2000, which was never even opened because it failed to obtain a safety certificate. Until 6 April 2009 the hospital didn't even appear on the property maps; as far as the state was concerned, the property did not exist. Construction had begun in 1972, but the work continually met with difficulty. In 1980, the same year as the earthquake in Irpinia, they were still working on the left side of the foundation. Following the earthquake, one of the labourers who had worked on the site, Pino, now nearly seventy years old, recalled how the hospital had been built: 'That concrete was water. On one side San Salvatore has pillars of sand.' Pino remembers reporting it to the unions, but a week later a union rep advised him to keep his mouth shut. During the earthquake an entire wing of San Salvatore Hospital collapsed and a large section of the building remained unfit for use.

Marco, Luciana, Angela, Francesco, Alessio, Davide, Michelone and Luca are not only victims of the earthquake, but also of human irresponsibility. Their tragedy is everyone's tragedy. In *One Hundred Years of Solitude*, Gabriel García Márquez writes that 'A person does not belong to a place until there is someone dead under the ground.' If you scroll through the names of children who lost their lives in the L'Aquila earthquake, it is immediately evident that a number of them are foreigners: 22 out of 308 victims. Antonio Ioavan Ghiroceanu is the youngest victim of the Abruzzo earthquake. He wasn't even five months old. Born in Italy, he was the son of Darinca and Laurentiu, a Romanian couple from Saint Demetrius. Children of Albanians, Romanians, Ukrainians, Moldavians who had come to Italy, to Abruzzo, seeking work and a better future. Marta and Ondreiy, aged sixteen and seventeen, had come to L'Aquila from the Czech Republic as a result of a travel award. They had been chosen as the best students at the Technical Institute of Pardubice, 90 kilometres from Prague.

When you die together it means you've lived together. Osmai Madi, a Macedonian mason, forty-two years old, lived in Poggio Picenze with his family. The earthquake caused his house to collapse. Osmai was able to save his wife and one daughter, but lost his other daughter, Valbona. In spite of that, realizing there was nothing more he could do for her, he went on to dig for others with his bare hands, to pull others out of the rubble. He saved eleven people of seven different nationalities.

It would be wonderful to imagine an Italy where earthquakes are not experienced as if they were happening for the first time, an Italy that's made better, constructed better, able to withstand seismic shocks. Instead we appear to relive the same tragedy each and every time. The anniversary of the earthquake in Irpinia has just passed and once again we seem to see the same things, hear about the same tragedies, feel the same despair, witness the same kickbacks and the same flaws and omissions. Some time ago I happened to read these words by the poet Franco Arminio of Campania, dedicated to victims of the earthquake in Irpinia, and I felt like I was revisiting what had happened in L'Aquila:

Conza della Campania, October 8, 2000
There are days when many people die. They are the days of great disasters. November 23, 1980 was such a day in this area.

Today is Sunday, in the cemetery of Conza it is eleven o'clock in the morning. Those who died in the earthquake are almost all in the same rows, a small cemetery within the cemetery. Faces of men and women of all ages. Faces and lives that I never knew. Now, for every person I see, I want to know what he said, what he did. From the photos adorning the headstones you can sometimes tell that they are individuals belonging to the same family. Here is Luisa Masini, nine years old, with a cat in her arms. Below her is Valeria Masini, twelve years old, then Maria, forty-three, their mother. Our thoughts fly immediately to the father: who knows where in the world he is, dragging along with his sorrow. Further on there's another family: Gino Ciccone, forty-nine, then Michele, age ten, and Alberto, twenty-one. Those who are here certainly all knew one another.

6.

The Mudslinging Machine

For some time now I've had a kind of obsession, an obsession that has to do with the mudslinging machine, a mechanism by which any individual may be smeared. And I have this obsession because I was born in a country in which anyone who has decided to thwart organized crime has always been subjected to this type of utter delegitimization. Even those who are killed, those who died opposing the Mafia, are vilified. So I'm sensitive to it: it's like I have an exposed nerve when it comes to this mechanism.

I feel that democracy is literally in danger. It may seem exaggerated, but it isn't. Democracy is in danger when what awaits you the moment you go up against certain powers, or take a stand against the government, is an attack from a machine that slings mud at you: an attack that starts with your private life, with minuscule facts about your private life which are used against you.

There is a difference between defamation and investigative reporting. An investigation gathers numerous pieces of evidence in order to reveal them to the reader. Journalists crave as much information as possible in order to dig more deeply, to find evidence that demonstrates, nails down, defends the facts. Those engaging in defamation on the other hand take an item out of context, a private matter that has no relation whatsoever with public affairs, and use it against the person whom they've decided to smear. Democracy is at risk when, at the time you turn on the computer to write your article, you think: 'Tomorrow they're going to attack me for things that have nothing to do with public life, nothing to do with any crime committed.' You haven't done anything wrong, but they will use your private life against you, force you to defend yourself. So, whoever you are, mayor, councilman, physician, journalist, think first before you criticize. When this happens, freedom of the press starts to crack, freedom of expression begins to crack.

Obviously, Italy isn't China, or a fascist dictatorship; no one is arrested for what he writes. But the confusion between defamation and investigation is a scheme. It is a way for those who smear others to defend themselves. The purpose is to be able to say: 'We're all alike.' In the end the mudslinging machine's strategy is to be able to say 'You do it too', 'We all do it.' And this technique works very well, because basically that's what people want to hear. Because, if we are all alike, no one needs to feel better than anyone else, or do anything to be better than anyone else. The mudslinging machine says we all have dirty hands, we're all the same.

The strength of democracy lies in diversity. But the instinct that is unfortunately emerging in the nation is to say: we're all alike, all identical, all one and the same. That's where the mudslinging machine wins. We must be able to spot differences. Difference is what the mudslinging machine doesn't want the viewer, the reader, the citizen to discern. Human weakness is one thing, crime is something else. A slip-up is one thing, extortion another matter. A politician can blunder, it means he's doing something. But a person who makes a misstep is very different from one who is corrupt.

In fact, when up against the mudslinging machine our response should not be to say: 'We're better.' Instead we should say: 'We're different.' We should emphasize the difference, not toss everything into the same kettle. Point out, for example, that privacy is sacred, that it's one of the pillars of democracy: being able to declare your feelings to the person you love without anyone overhearing you. I often use this example to show the boundaries that are invaded by being observed, by gossip that becomes a tool for blackmail: imagine what it would mean to be photographed while in the toilet. We all go to the bathroom, we all sit on the toilet bowl, there's nothing wrong with that. But if someone photographs you there and circulates a photo of that universal act, you lose credibility because, when you talk, the people you meet – your neighbours, your listeners if you have a public presence – will always remember that picture, that image. Yet you've done nothing wrong.

It is important to understand there are limits that are the foundation of democracy. It's one thing to make a declaration of love, another to nominate your friends for office because you like them and then end up a possible victim of blackmail and extortion. The latter ceases to be a private matter because it becomes an influence on the life of the entire country. The first instance, privacy, is a desire to live; the second is an abuse of power. The difference is critical, because the objective of the mudslinging machine is to say: it's all the same thing. And, most importantly, lower your eyes, don't criticize, let the shrewdest one win and, if you criticize, this is what you can expect: your entire private life will be made public.

What happens in Italy when you irritate those in power? Machinery is activated, made up of dossiers, conspiring journalists and shady politicians who try to discredit their rivals through blackmail and the media. I could tell you a lot of stories. The one about the Monte Carlo home of Gianfranco Fini, chairman of the Chamber of Deputies, which started when he began to disagree with several positions held by his party. But where was the crime? It was an inelegant, inappropriate move. But there was no crime. I could tell you the story about Dino Boffo, editor of the Catholic newspaper *Avvenire*, who had timidly begun to criticize Berlusconi's conduct. The mudslinging machine hinted that it was in possession of a document of a judicial nature which read: 'Known homosexual, under surveillance by the police.' But what was the crime, homosexuality? I could tell you that the alleged homosexuality of Stefano Caldoro became a weapon used by his party colleague, Nicola Cosentino, to take his place as candidate for governor of Campania.

How is it conceivable that homosexuality might be considered a crime? How is it possible to think of using it as delegitimization? In actuality such misinformation is more than mere calumny, which is used mainly against enemies. Misinformation is aimed at destroying victims from within their own side; it is used as punishment, to force you to defend yourself to those close to you, to make statements that have nothing to do with your public activity. It sows doubts and insinuates suspicions that even friends begin to fear. Whatever your lifestyle, whatever work you do, whatever your thinking is, if you oppose certain powers they will always respond with a single strategy: to delegitimize you.

The mudslinging machine wasn't born today; it's been at work for some time. That's why I would like to tell the story of a man who endured and survived the mudslinging machine and in the end could only be stopped by explosives. This man's name was Giovanni Falcone.

In 1983 Rocco Chinnici is killed. An anti-mafia magistrate and a courageous man, he too was a victim of delegitimization: twenty-four hours after his execution, he was said to have been killed over a romantic matter. As a result of this homicide, the investigative branch of the Prosecution Office in Palermo falls under the supervision of Justice Antonino Caponnetto, who decides to establish an anti-mafia pool composed of magistrates who will be assigned full-time and exclusively to Mafia trials. Called upon to be part of the pool are Giovanni Falcone, Paolo Borsellino, Giuseppe Di Lello and Leonardo Guarnotta. This pool forever changes the world's judicial history, because it succeeds in addressing the issue of crime not only as a matter of safety, but as a factor in the Western economy. The judges confront the issue, study it, understand its codes, and manage to conclude the biggest trial against the Mafia that has ever been brought: nineteen life sentences for all members of the *cupola*, the body of top-ranking Mafia bosses, and 2,665 years of prison for 339 defendants. In short, thanks to this pool, Italy discovers that it has definitive formal evidence of the existence of the Cosa Nostra.

The judges' work is intense and very dangerous, and for this reason a strong system of protection is mobilized, drawing criticism from the newspapers. The press attacks the anti-mafia pool and it attacks Giovanni Falcone. Instead of being proud of the judges, it isolates them. People are afraid or, worse yet, fed up with this war fought in their own city. The deployment of forces is perceived as an inconvenience and people seem to consider what is happening a kind of private battle between Falcone and the Cosa Nostra.

A letter is sent to the *Giornale di Sicilia* in April 1985 by a reader complaining about the racket caused by the security measures taken to protect the magistrates:

> Regularly, every day of the week (never mind Saturday or Sunday), morning, noon, afternoon or evening (no matter what time), I am literally 'assaulted' by the constant, deafening sirens of police cars escorting the various judges. Now I ask you: how can a person possibly get a little rest during her time off from work, or at least watch a television programme in peace, when even with the windows closed, the noise of the sirens is so loud? I ask you: why don't they build villas for these 'illustrious gentlemen' in the outskirts of the city?

Villas in the outskirts of the city. Why don't you people go and fight your battles someplace else, outside the city? The lady writing the letter is not a mafiosa, but she considers the fight against the Mafia pointless. After all, obeying the Mafia is very simple: if you don't cross them, you get what you've been promised. With the government it's more complicated: often you don't get what the law should provide, and it's harder to lead a life consistent with lawful principles, especially in the South. Falcone and the anti-mafia pool immediately come under attack. Falcone is accused of being a *carrierista*, a careerist, an opportunist who does what he does to enhance his own personal power. The same *Giornale di Sicilia* writes in 1986:

The comical figures of bizarre judges who populate the judiciary proscenium of our times: the judge who, wearing a bulletproof vest, pistol in hand, swoops in with his helicopter, seizes thousands of documents, then vanishes over the horizon like a white knight [. . .] the one who, leading dozens and dozens of armed troops, storms the location of the blitz of the day, after making sure that the press was tipped off beforehand [. . .] or the judge who offers the defence attorney a passport or some other favour, if his client will only decide to cooperate. [. . .]

Are those real judges? [. . .] If he weren't dashing around, tyres squealing in his armoured Alfetta, surrounded by TV cameras and floodlights, if the poor judge, sitting alone, bent over the bound volumes of the penal code, were to see to it that the rules, that is, the parties' rights, were respected in the trials, he would not have the benefit of publicity nor, alas, of official merit and recognition.

It is important to remember these words because today we tend to think that Giovanni Falcone was supported in his battle from the outset. In fact, he never was, except by a very few. Those who take a stand against the Mafia, and especially those with Falcone's skills, face the usual accusation: 'You're doing it for your own interest, you're doing it because you think you're better than us.' The *Giornale di Sicilia,* in November 1986, carries a headline asking whether the fight against the Mafia is becoming a huge spectacle.

Even an intellectual like Leonardo Sciascia falls for it. In December 1986, Paolo Borsellino is elected chief prosecutor of the Public Prosecution Office in Marsala, beating the other candidate, Giuseppe Alcamo. Borsellino's professionalism, demonstrated in the huge criminal trial against the Mafia, which took place at that time, dubbed the Maxi Trial, prevails over Alcamo's seniority. It is a strong decision, which goes against the judiciary's hardened tradition of assigning appointments based on length of service. The event does not go unnoticed. A few days later an article by Sciascia appears in the *Corriere della Sera*, entitled 'Anti-Mafia Professionals'; in it the writer takes a critical stance towards those who distinguish themselves through their efforts against the Cosa Nostra, judging this phenomenon to be a kind of professionalism for career advancement purposes. 'Anti-Mafia Professionals' will become somewhat of a manifesto for those who revile the anti-mafia pool from that time on. Sciascia later acknowledged the short-sightedness of that assessment and stated that he had been misinformed. The danger he had glimpsed was that of an anti-mafia battle that might be all form and no content.

That's the kind of thing Falcone and the other members of the pool had to endure for many long years. A scene that has always struck me is the day Antonino Caponnetto retires. His natural successor as head of the Prosecution Office in Palermo would be Giovanni Falcone. Antonino Meli, the public prosecutor in Caltanissetta, a magistrate at the end of his career, also submits his candidacy. A good man, no question, but lacking Falcone's skills and strength. Once again, as with Borsellino in Marsala, it is merit acquired in the field versus length of service. Victory this time, however, is not awarded to the best candidate: fourteen votes for Meli, ten for Falcone. Five abstentions. Falcone's disappointment and that of his supporters is enormous. It is not a conflict between two individuals but between two ways of viewing the Mafia. Falcone knows that Caponnetto's departure means the end of the pool, and on that day he can't hold back tears. He weeps in public because he can't stand

thinking about all those who had died, the police and carabinieri who had been killed, he can't stand the idea that everything
they had done was coming to an end because of a bureaucratic
decision.

Being passed over internally weakens Falcone and encourages
an outburst of external delegitimization. The anti-mafia magistrates are treated like superstars on the covers of illustrated
magazines. Falcone is described as 'supermagistrate', 'super-
escorted', 'a legend', 'a phenomenon', 'Falconcrest'. 'Dangerous
political tendencies of the left' are attributed to him and he is
accused of being a communist supporter.

Thus begins a steady trickle that reaches a crescendo in
Addaura. In the summer of 1989 Falcone is vacationing in this
small seaside town near Palermo. He is investigating money
laundering by the Cosa Nostra. On 20 June an agent of his escort
unit finds a bag full of explosives hidden among the rocks where
the magistrate usually goes to swim: it is immediately clear that
this is an assassination attempt. Falcone isn't surprised, he's been
expecting it. He knows he is isolated and he knows the more
secluded he is, the more his life is in danger. But even the failed
assassination attempt becomes an occasion for defamation: in the
parlours of Palermo they say that he himself had the bomb
planted, in order to attract attention to himself and advance his
career. They say: the Mafia doesn't make mistakes, the Mafia
doesn't warn you, it kills you and that's that. Which is to say: you
yourself staged the assassination attempt.

Falcone knew Italy and was well aware of the formula by
which if the mafia doesn't kill you, if the attempt fails, you risk
losing credibility. He knew that in Italy only death can legitimize
you. Here's what he is asked in a television broadcast hosted by
Corrado Augias: 'You say in your book that in Sicily one dies
because one is alone. Since you are happily still with us, who pro-
tects you?' Falcone responds with: 'Must one be killed in order to
be credible in this country? This blessed country where, if they

plant a bomb near your house and the bomb luckily doesn't explode, it's your fault that you didn't make it explode.'

These words are chilling. Because they are true. The 'blessed' country Falcone is talking about is the somewhat superficial country that thinks it can talk about anything and easily dismiss it: if they want to kill you, they kill you. That's how Falcone becomes isolated, because in the meantime the Cosa Nostra gets stronger and stronger; it fattens up and leaves the dirty work to its envious colleagues, to citizens' groups, to those who can't stand what Falcone is doing. In other words, it turns the anti-mafia battle into a *societal* battle. It then becomes very easy, like going out on a Saturday night, seeing a person on the ground and saying, 'Oh well, he deserves it, he's plastered.' And you don't feel compelled to help him, because if you do you'll ruin your Saturday night. Similarly it is easier to say that people like Falcone are out to further their career, that those who do these things do it for money or greater glory. It's better that way. Because if you believe they are doing the right thing, if you believe they are competent, then you have to follow them. And if you do not, you become complicit. That's the 'blessed' country where, if you don't die, you're guilty because you're alive.

The summer of 1989 is 'the summer of poison-pens'. Following the distrust shown towards the authenticity of the assassination attempt in Addaura, six anonymous letters from '*Corvo*', the Crow, addressed to different public figures, are disclosed. One of these letters is to Achille Occhetto, then secretary of the Communist Party, who is put on guard by Falcone's apparent about-turn. The accusation here is that he sold out: 'Until today, Giovanni Falcone, to put it mildly, was putting one over on you, making you believe that he's an anti-mafia white knight whereas he's shown himself to be a sleazy opportunist. [. . .] In short, Falcone sold out for the position of deputy prosecutor.'

True, Falcone became deputy prosecutor in Palermo, but his life became a living hell. Letters from the 'Crow' arrive monthly, in an attempt to ignite even greater anger. At the Prosecutor's Office he's kept waiting. When you work in the same office and you have to see your boss, if there's a collaborative relationship you knock and enter. When you're made to step aside instead, when you have to have the secretary announce you, you're kept waiting with the attorneys who may be representing the same people whom you've put on trial. Everyone sees you waiting there for hours before the chief prosecutor receives you. And that is meant to convey that the prosecutor is no longer of the same mind, he has other priorities.

Falcone is assigned trials that are inconsequential. His former Sicilian supporters criticize his methods in the investigations and his conduct is viewed as a betrayal, as caving in and investigating on the 'third level', the political level of Mafia control. He is accused of hiding away in drawers documents that would lead to the solving of prominent homicides. If at the time of the Palermo anti-mafia pool he was accused of being a friend of the communists, now he is branded as a friend of Andreotti, the former Prime Minister who was tried and acquitted for Mafia association. In Rome there are those who say that he no longer fights on the front line. On 29 October 1991 the journalist Lino Jannuzzi comments on Falcone's candidacy as head of the *Direzione nazionale antimafia* (National Anti-Mafia Directorate), calling him 'one of those most responsible for the state's debacle with regard to the Mafia':

> Starting today, or tomorrow, we will have to watch out for two Cosa Nostras, the one whose *cupola* is in Palermo and the one about to be installed in Rome. And you'd be wise to keep your passport handy.

Articles appear branding Falcone as 'more a manager than a magistrate now'. Attention is drawn to his excessive television presence. In short, he is not forgiven for being a public figure.

Only his actions are attacked, rather than the facts: Sandro Viola calls him a 'TV minstrel'.

The attacks from the left become more violent when, in March 1991, Falcone is called to Rome by Minister of Justice Claudio Martelli, to serve as director of the Criminal Affairs division: now he's not only a friend of Andreotti but also of the Socialists. Now he's in the 'palace of power', he's the 'prince's adviser'. And this is worrisome because, with politics presumably compromising the institutions, the independence of the judiciary might be in danger. Obviously Falcone is well aware of the history of the Christian Democrats, their relations with the Cosa Nostra in Sicily. But he accepts the position in Rome just the same, because his role is an administrative one, not a political one. Falcone has confidence in the institutions and knows that, if an institution is strong, it is stronger than politics, it is a guarantee of democracy. So he keeps doing what he knows how to: serving the state, that is, enabling the state to develop an office that will coordinate the battle against organized crime.

But the left slaughters him: you're collaborating! On 26 September 1991, during a TV special about the killing of Libero Grassi, on the talk show *Samarcanda*, attorney Alfredo Galasso, a Palermo criminal lawyer who fought on the same anti-mafia front with Falcone, attacks him on this very issue:

GALASSO: If you ask me Giovanni Falcone would be well advised to leave the ministerial halls as soon as possible, because it seems to me that the air there is not good for him.

FALCONE: That's your subjective opinion, indicating the lack of a sense of state.

GALASSO: On the contrary, to me it seems like what's lacking is a sense of the independence and autonomy of the judiciary.

FALCONE: The post I hold is intended for judges, it has nothing to do with the independence of the judiciary. In any country in the world there is a Ministry of Justice, in any country in the world there are judges who are in the ministry. You're confusing independence with irresponsibility and licence.

GALASSO: Independence for me is very specific: not having to answer to anyone, either before, during or after.

FALCONE: That's the problem: those who are independent always have to answer for it.

GALASSO: Not judges.

FALCONE: How can you say that? There's an excellent law on civil responsibility, and you say they're not responsible?

GALASSO: Judges answer to the people in whose name they administer justice. And for that reason there is a sovereign body like the Supreme Judicial Council which, in the name of the people, must ensure this independence. In any case, Giovanni, I don't like you being inside the halls of government, I don't like it.

Attorney Galasso is a decent man. He expresses what the left was thinking, and sometimes still thinks: you're being a collaborator, being inside and reforming things. Purity has been the greatest space compromised to enemies of democracy and criminal organizations. 'I'm pure, I don't dirty my hands.' But that way Falcone's left on his own. He turns away with some bitterness and lets it go. A statesman knows what his mission is: the institution. It's not about politics. In Rome, Falcone works on the *Superprocura* (Super-prosecutor) project, the creation of a body to coordinate anti-mafia investigations throughout the country. It will serve to establish the National Anti-Mafia Prosecutor's Office, which still exists today, because Falcone, who was not only a great intellectual but also a great magistrate, understood that the battle against the Mafia must be won on a national and international level, not at the local level.

Even in this case they attack him, continuing to accuse him of not being independent from politics and of having been appointed only because he's famous. The daily *Il Resto del Carlino* carries the headline 'Falcone, undeserved fame', and goes on:

Untrustworthy and Martelli-dependent. [. . .] He was just one component (the most famous one) of Palermo's anti-mafia pool. [. . .] All Falcone did was add his signature. The indictments are the work of those in charge of the maxi-trials.

What they're telling him is: you're not even proficient, you're just famous.

What had been one of the strengths of the anti-mafia pool? Communication. They conducted an all-out blitz, and the newspapers talked about it. There was a chance to communicate and Falcone went for it. They never forgave him for the fact that these stories weren't relegated to the shadows in prosecutors' offices, or confined to the local news, but reached everyone. Paolo Borsellino reported that Falcone once said: 'I have a feeling that people are rooting for us, that things are changing.' For that he was not forgiven.

There is an episode that explains better than any other Falcone's state of mind during this period. It occurs on the day of his death, 23 May 1992. Falcone is in the car with his wife and driver on the road leading from Punta Raisi airport to Palermo. They've returned from Rome to go to Favignana, to see the *mattanza*, the traditional tuna slaughter. Falcone likes to drive and this time he himself is at the wheel, with an escort car in front and one behind. His usual driver says, 'Afterwards you can give me the car keys, Sir, or take them up to the house with you.' Falcone is so lost in thought that he takes the keys out while the car is running, killing the engine. The car stalls. 'We'll get ourselves killed this way,' the driver tells us he said. Meanwhile Giovanni Brusca, thinking that they have noticed something, pushes the button ahead of time and sets off the bomb. Over a thousand pounds of TNT wipes out the first car, the one carrying the escort. The second car is sent flying against the asphalt, which has heaved up. Only the driver is saved and it is from him that we know the details about the last moments of Falcone's life.

For the first time the critics stop. Falcone's death does away with the controversy. He becomes a hero. Almost as though death were the only possible evidence of the authenticity of his battle against the Mafia. But we must not forget. We must not forget that they slandered him, delegitimized him. When we realize that power delegitimizes, let's not fall for it. All we have to do is say: 'This is mud, it doesn't interest me, I won't listen to it.'

In an interview in *La Repubblica* marking the tenth anniversary of Falcone's death, Milan prosecutor Ilda Boccassini recalled how greatly Giovanni Falcone had been attacked in life and how greatly eulogized after his death:

No man in Italy has accumulated more defeats in his life than Falcone. [. . .] Criticized as an investigating magistrate. Criticized as prosecutor in Palermo. Criticized as a candidate for the Council of Magistrates. And he would have been criticized as the national anti-mafia prosecutor as well, if he had not been killed. [. . .] And yet [. . .] every year we celebrate Giovanni's life as if he had been awarded public recognition or esteemed for his excellence. Another paradox. No man has had his trust and friendship betrayed with greater determination and malice.

These words should never leave our minds. They have never left my heart at any rate. Because it is important to remember what was done to a talented man, and it is especially important to remember him when things go wrong, when you don't think you can make it, when you have the feeling that the worst individuals always advance, when you're afraid to step forward for fear of becoming the target of the mudslinging machine. At difficult moments like that I think about the skill and strength of Giovanni Falcone, a man who, despite defeats, despite betrayals, never stopped believing in the power of the law. The dream of a different Italy was the energy that made him feel alive. All the friends and journalists who were close to him say that Falcone loved life, he wanted to live. But he knew that you can only be happy if others can be happy too. And that the law is the only premise for happiness.

7

Piero and Mina

It may be somewhat unusual for me, but I would like to tell you a love story that got to me, and hasn't left me. Which is what happens with meaningful stories that you read or hear about.

It is the spring of 1973. A long time ago, before I was born. A girl on an excursion with her parish, a young woman from Alto Adige, gets lost in the streets of Rome, perhaps the biggest city she's ever been to in her life. She has to get to Piazza Venezia and Campo de' Fiori, and doesn't know the way. She sees a gentleman sitting nearby and asks him for directions. The young man is wearing a fringed jacket and has long blond hair. He looks like a hippie. He stands up; he's very tall, over six feet. He not only gives her directions, but offers to walk her there. She notices that he's limping and tells him: 'No need, I'll find it by myself.' 'No, I'll walk you.' And so Piergiorgio Welby and Wilhelmine Schett, known as Mina, head towards Piazza Venezia together. On the way, they talk about everything you can possibly talk about in just a few minutes. He, a worldly protester from '68, has toured Europe, writes and paints. She, a practising Catholic, on a parish trip to Rome. Yet these two worlds, so seemingly distant, come together.

When they say goodbye, they exchange phone numbers and addresses. They start writing to each other, learning about one another. Piero cannot forget that girl from Alto Adige, though he only saw her for a few minutes. Mina too has not forgotten Piero, so she returns to Rome, this time for him. She will never leave, because Piero immediately suggests that they live together in the house he shares with his parents. Things go smoothly, as is the case when something new is being born.

After two years of living together, Piero's mother takes the opportunity at supper to ask: 'Why don't you two get married?' Piero is silent; Mina keeps her eyes lowered and Piero changes the subject. The evening comes to an end. When they are alone, however, Mina asks him: 'Why didn't you answer? Don't you want to marry me?' Piero replies: 'I don't want to marry you. Because you must be free, free to leave whenever you want. When my illness turns me into a lifeless stump, I will only be a burden to you.'

Piero has already explained that he suffers from progressive muscular dystrophy, a neuro-degenerative disease that affects the muscles and progressively destroys the body. But it is only then that he confides his fears to her: 'I can't hide anything from you, I will die asphyxiated.' Mina replies with disarming simplicity, a simplicity as deep as the sea: 'In the meantime we can carry on. After all, no one knows what the future holds. Those who are afraid of the future don't live in the present.' And so, with her simplicity, she completely defuses the dramatic charge of Piero's words, spoken to avoid jeopardizing Mina's happiness.

In 1980 they get married in church, since the Welby family is Catholic. Piero arrives at the wedding in a wheelchair; the disease is slowly affecting everything: arms, hands, legs, even the heart. He used to love walking in the woods because his father was a hunter, but he can't do it anymore. Mina does not lose heart and with her usual simplicity tells him: 'If you can't go hunting anymore, we'll go fishing!' That's how Mina is: for her, the fact that you can no longer do something is merely a reason to do other things that may be even more enjoyable and entertaining. And so they go fishing, Piero in the wheelchair, with the fishing rods in a pole holder mounted on the chair. And, since Piero has difficulty moving his arms, Mina also learns how to bait the hook: 'I never in my life imagined that I would end up putting worms on a hook.'

For Mina especially, but also for Piero, all of the hurdles that arise, and there are many, always seem to be opportunities to come up with an alternative way of living. As if every obstacle were a necessary step to put their feelings to the test and above all to build something solid, not something that is merely a way of coping with a tragedy. To create a life for themselves. Because of the respirator, Piero can no longer leave the house. So Mina tries to bring the nature that he loved so much home to him. They devise a way of photographing insects, flowers, flies ... They never photograph dead insects, only those that are still alive! Mina helps Piero understand that the present is the only true form of eternity that man can know. Piero will tell her: 'You made me do so many things that I didn't even realize I was ill.'

They had made a pact, Mina and Piero: if he were to worsen, she would not bring him to the hospital. Piero thought that he would go into a coma and then die. She promises, but then that dreadful day arrives, the terrifying respiratory crisis, and Mina, frightened, cannot do it. She cannot accept the idea of losing him and calls an ambulance. It's one thing to make a pact, another to go through with it. Piero undergoes a tracheotomy: a surgical incision is made in his trachea to open an alternative airway to the natural one, and from that day on he will live attached to a ventilator, immobile, in bed. This artificial respirator is a device that inflates and deflates, pumping air into the body. Its measured sound is similar to the piston of a locomotive.

But their life does not stop. Piero read a lot, he devoured books. He would listen to a programme about books, *Fahrenheit*, on RadioTre, oxygen for every reader, and then he'd say to Mina: 'I want this book. But we have no money.' And Mina would joke: 'But you're rich, that's why I married you!' In reality they lived on a disability allowance of 450,000 liras a month, which today would be around 500 euros.

Piero also loves to paint: oil paintings. At first for pleasure: the chance to create, to take his mind off things. But as the disease progresses, his movements become increasingly difficult, so he asks Mina to shift the canvas under his hands according to the figure he wants to paint, while he holds the brush steady between his fingers. Mina then suggests that he paint smaller pictures: 'Even the great artists have done it.' In fact, his last works are small in size. Mina hoped that all this would allow him to remain attached to life. In her book she writes: 'I really employed extraordinary lifesaving measures, but these extreme measures were a form of love.'

In 2001 the disease worsens and Piero loses heart. 'It's all over,' he says. 'Enough.' Muscular dystrophy is a disease that destroys the body while, in most cases, leaving the mind intact. The patient is therefore absolutely lucid, conscious of wasting away and aware of his suffering. Piero asks his wife to support him in his request to disconnect the respirator. Mina gets angry, she cannot accept it, for her it's as if he were saying that he wants to leave her. It's as if he were telling her: 'I don't love you anymore.' And so her response is: 'I won't give you a divorce!' Then Piero, who knows her so well, calls her over as he always does by clicking his tongue, and asks her to put her hands around his neck. 'Come on now, don't be like that, I understand completely.' Mina often says: 'I was his nurse, he was my psychologist; he always knew how to handle me.' Mina thought it was Piergiorgio who was being self-centred, but later she comes to realize that she was the self-centred one.

Piero then begins the battle, along with the Radical Party, for permission to disconnect the respirator. In 2002 he begins writing a blog, which he will update constantly until the final day of his life. He writes under the pseudonym of Caliban, the character in Shakespeare's *The Tempest*: a monster, a deformed, freckled savage 'not honoured with a human shape'. Through this forum he comes into contact with people from all over the world who have the same urgency he has, who are experiencing the same suffering that he is.

Piero wants to get quickly to what he calls a 'dignified death', doing everything within the law. What he's asking for is not euthanasia, that is, the practice of bringing about the death of a human being suffering from an incurable disease as painlessly and swiftly as possible, without bloodshed, in order to put an end to his suffering. He's asking for the law to forgo extraordinary lifesaving measures, namely, all those medical techniques that serve to artificially maintain the vital functions of patients with incurable diseases. He doesn't want to shorten his life by causing his own death. As Cardinal Carlo Maria Martini puts it: 'By declining artificial life support, he's not trying to cause his death, but accepting the fact that he can't stop it.' People who go to see him, not understanding this, say to Mina: 'He wants to die because he's dejected, because he's not getting the proper care.'

On 22 September 2006, Piero decides to send a video-letter to the President of the Republic, Giorgio Napolitano. By now he's become accustomed to using a speech synthesizer: on the monitor in front of him are letters, which he indicates with his eyes, and the synthesizer produces the words he wants to say. His message is the poetic manifesto of his battle for life:

> I love life, Mr President. Life is the woman who loves you, the wind through your hair, the sun on your face, an evening stroll with a friend. Life is also a woman who leaves you, a rainy day, a friend who deceives you. I am neither melancholic nor manic depressive. I find the idea of dying horrible, but what is left to me is no longer a life . . . it is only a stubborn and senseless obstinacy of keeping active the biological functions.

They are beautiful words, which not only pertain to the question of bioethics, but reveal wisdom. The wind in your hair, the woman you love, but also the woman who leaves you, the friend who betrays you: here is a man who does not see life solely as a happy journey. 'I find the idea of dying horrible,' he says. He is afraid, but he does not want to resort to suicide, he doesn't even think about it. He no longer considers his life a form of living. What others may consider life, for Piero isn't. And he feels that he alone has the one and only right to decide his fate. He feels he has that right.

Piergiorgio Welby's strength, and that of Beppino Englaro and Luca Coscioni, who have also fought for the right to die, is to have acted within the law, to have always claimed the right to decide. Piero could have gone to Switzerland, and Mina had once suggested it to him: 'There it's allowed, there is no artificial life support, there they put you to sleep.' He had replied: 'And what if the plane crashes?' Because his objective was not only to resolve a personal issue, but to establish the right to die within the law. Piero, Beppino and Luca could easily have paid an inducement, as people in fact do in Italian hospitals. Euthanasia already exists: you pay someone to act in silence. This too was proposed to Mina: 'You stop feeding him and over time he weakens . . .'

That's why the words of Piergiorgio Welby to President Napolitano are words that affect not only the patient's rights, but the rights of all Italians. Because each time we claim the right to make our own personal choices, we are safeguarding the rights of everyone.

A doctor in Cremona, an anaesthesiologist named Mario Riccio who had followed the Welby story in the newspapers and listened to the words addressed to the President of the Republic, decides to assist Piero. It's just a few days before Christmas and he says to him: 'So then, see you after Christmas?' Piero already feels it's all over, all he wants is for this final door to open and for it to be a normal moment for him, so he responds decisively: 'No, no, I'll see you on Wednesday, after the Deal or no Deal.'

On the afternoon of that 20 December, Mina is sad. Everything she does for him, ordinary things she's done for so many years, makes her think: 'I'm doing this for the last time.' Overcome by anxiety, she's frenetic. He asks her: 'Have you been happy?' One of those questions you'd always like to ask the person you love. For Mina it had been 'a full and happy life, the best I could have imagined'. And so she tells him: 'Come and take me with you, what will I do without you?' 'You'll have plenty to do!' he makes light of it.

It is that afternoon that Piero confesses to Mina: 'Dying is no joke.' On the evening of his last day, he checks his e-mails, responds to comments on the blog and then deletes everything. Around eleven o'clock, Piergiorgio says goodbye to the relatives and three of the Radical friends gathered at his bedside. The doctor approaches and asks: 'Shall we proceed?' For this last response Piero wants to use his voice. Breathless, he says 'Yes.' Mina then asks him: 'Do you really want to?' Piero blinks, just once, meaning 'Yes.' He dies shortly afterward, in the dignified manner he had requested and desired for so long, in compliance with the law.

Being a Catholic, as is Piero's mother, Mina wants to observe the final obsequies in a church. However, she receives this reply from the Vicar's office in Rome:

> With regard to the request for ecclesiastical funeral rites for the late Mr. Piergiorgio Welby, the Vicariate of Rome informs you that it cannot grant such rites because, unlike suicide cases in which the absence of the circumstances of full awareness and deliberate consent is assumed, Mr Welby's resolve to put an end to his own life was known; it was repeatedly and publicly affirmed, which is in conflict with Catholic doctrine.

This response comes from the same institution that ensured a regular burial for Enrico De Pedis, known as Renatino, a boss who was one of the founders of the Magliana gang, killed near Campo de' Fiori in Rome on 2 February 1990 by hitmen sent by his 'former friends'. His name is linked to the story of Emanuela Orlandi, the girl who went missing in the Vatican in 1983. Renatino never served a day in prison and his body lies in the crypt of the Basilica of Sant'Apollinare in Rome. After he was entombed, the keys of the gate were entrusted to his widow Carla; only she is allowed access. Catholic funerals were also granted to dictators such as Francisco Franco and Augusto Pinochet. Franco, who established in Spain a regime backed by Nazi Germany and fascist Italy, the man responsible for the deaths of more than 250,000 people who opposed his government, is venerated as a saint by the Palmarian church, a schismatic Catholic sect. At the religious ceremony in honour of Pinochet, the former Chilean dictator convicted of crimes against humanity, 60,000 people paid homage to the body. In March 1991, Mario Iovine, one of the founders of the Casalesi clan, was buried with religious rites in Casal di Principe, at night. At the funeral of Roberto Sannolla, a mafioso from the Apulian organization, *Sacra corona unita*, killed while hiding out in Montenegro, girls dressed as brides followed the bier.

All religious, Catholic funerals. The church where Mina wanted to say a last farewell to Piero remained closed, however. The funeral service for Piergiorgio Welby was a civil ceremony held in the square across from the church of San Giovanni Bosco in Rome. A religious funeral, granted to dictators and criminals, to people who took the lives of others, was denied to Piergiorgio Welby, a just man whose only sin was to decide – after having endured his disease for forty years – that he didn't want to suffer anymore, that he wanted to take control of his own life. At the funeral it was recalled that Piero had simply wanted to stop the torment; all he had asked for was a final act of love.

The love of Mina and Piero had started in Campo de' Fiori, beneath the statue of Giordano Bruno, the philosopher born in Nola, in Campania. For me that statue is now no longer just the statue of a philosopher whom I esteem, a beacon of philosophical thought. It is also a reminder of Mina and Piero's love story. Now when I read the last words of Giordano Bruno, I think of Piergiorgio Welby:

I struggled, and greatly: I thought I could win (but my limbs lacked the strength of my soul), and fate and nature held back my study and my efforts. [. . .] As far as I am concerned, I did my best [. . .]: not fearing death, not yielding, standing firm, to any equal, preferring a courageous death to a noncombative life.

8.

Democracy Bought and Sold and the Ship of the Constitution

At the end of 2010 students all across Italy took to the streets to protest against the university reform proposed by the Minister of Education, Mariastella Gelmini. They occupied some of the foremost Italian monuments: the Tower of Pisa, the Colosseum in Rome, the Mole Antonelliana in Turin and the Basilica of St Anthony in Padua. Places that are symbolic of Italy. Their actions were intended to rouse the country from more than ten years of slumber, from the myopia that has prevented it from believing and investing in Italy's greatest endowment, which is culture and erudition. It is as if they had wanted to send this message: 'The Italy we yearn for, that we dream of, that we want to try to build, must start out from these places.' It was a gesture at once new and age-old: delving into Italy's history to seek continuity and consequently a different future. Taking control of the future by reclaiming the past, by recouping Italy's bygone treasures.

One of the treasures of our nation is the Italian Constitution. It may seem like a stock phrase, the kind of thing your grandparents might say when they're trying to teach you. Nevertheless I realized that it was actually true when I read the speech about the Constitution that Piero Calamandrei delivered to students at the University of Milan in 1955. In this speech Calamandrei, a member of the Constituent Assembly and one of the fathers of the Constitution, says that the Constitution 'is not a machine that once it has been started it goes on by itself. The Constitution is a piece of paper: I drop it and it doesn't move. To make it move you need to put in fuel every day, you need to put in your commitment, your spirit, your will to keep these promises, your sense of responsibility.' The Constitution as a covenant, then, to be forever and continually kept alive through our own sense of duty.

Perhaps the revolt of the Italian universities was aimed squarely at defending the Constitution. Article 34 speaks of the right to education:

> Capable and deserving pupils, including those lacking financial resources, have the right to attain the highest levels of education.

In legal terms the Constitution is the first principle. A nation should aspire to move towards the realization of the principles contained in it. Whether you are on the right or on the left, the Constitution is both a starting point and a destination. A way of saying: this is how we want to be, let's try to be that way.

What is the duty of the Republic in all this? Calamandrei cites Article 3:

> It is the duty of the Republic to remove those obstacles of an economic or social nature which constrain the freedom and equality of citizens, thereby impeding the full development of the human person and the effective participation of all workers in the political, economic and social organization of the country.

Calamandrei added:

> It is the task (of the Republic) to remove the obstacles that forbid the full development of the human being. Therefore, give everybody a job, give everybody a fair wage, give everybody an education, give all men the dignity of human beings. Only when this is achieved will we be able to say that the content of the first article, 'Italy is a democratic Republic, founded on labour', has become a reality. Because unless every person has the possibility

of working and studying and of drawing security from his/her job the means of living as a human being, not only our Republic won't be able to be called 'founded on labour', but we won't even be able to call it democratic, because a democracy in which there isn't this real equality, in which there is only an equality of right, is merely a formal democracy. It is not a democracy in which all the citizens can really contribute to the life of society, to give their best contribution, in which all the spiritual forces of all the citizens can be used to contribute to this process, to this constant progress, of the whole society.

Indifference to politics, non-participation: that's the danger that Calamandrei feared. And in the end this is precisely the aim of the mudslinging machine, of the ruthless mechanism of delegitimization. To get us to say 'They are all alike', 'We are all alike.' Responding to the failure of the political system by generalizing, by saying 'We are all alike', is the fastest way to sink the ship on which we all find ourselves.

Calamandrei uses the metaphor of the boat, the ship, and it is a metaphor that I have always found very apt. It is expressed in the story of two immigrants, two peasants, who are crossing the ocean on a lurching ship. One of the peasants is asleep in the hold, the other is on deck and sees that there is a huge storm brewing, with towering waves that are causing the ship to pitch. Frightened, he asks a seaman: 'Are we in danger?' The seaman replies: 'If these swells continue, the ship will sink in half an hour.' So the peasant runs down to the hold to wake his companion and cries: 'Beppe, Beppe, if these swells continue, the ship will sink in half an hour.' And his friend says: 'What do I care, it's not mine!' That's what indifference is, that's what non-participation means. But not participating, believing that what's happening around you doesn't concern you, entails handing over the country to powers that know how to organize and manage consensus, and who will take away everything you have. To think of the state as something apart from us means losing the prospect of law. The state is not apart from us, the state is us.

Seemingly the consequences are not all negative. For example, you can use politics to get what the law does not grant you. If you don't have a job, you strive to get one by voting for a certain politician; if you don't have a good bed in the hospital, you vote for the councilman who will do you a favour and obtain one for you. This is what politics is likely to become when there is no participation by everyone: no respect for fundamental rights anymore, simply a matter of trading favours. What is hard to understand is that all this seems reasonable. To all appearances it appears so, but in reality it isn't. Because the politician who promises you favours, while giving you one thing, takes away all the rest. He gives you a hospital bed for your grandmother, maybe he gives you a permit to open a tobacco shop, he gives you a poorly paid job off the books, but he's taking away everything else. He takes away the possibility of breathing clean air, he takes away the work you deserve if you are capable. He takes away the schools to which you should have a right.

I've often wondered: how much does a vote cost? Every time there is an election, in the hours preceding the announcement of the final results, we often wonder: Who won? Which regions were the determining factor? Sometimes we wonder how those votes were obtained, whether they were bought. But how much does a vote cost? It's simple. During the period of the 2010 regional elections, the Naples District Anti-Mafia Directorate began an investigation into vote-buying. In Campania, prices were found to range from 20 to 50 euros, 25 up front and 25 on balance, that is, after the vote is cast. In some cases, votes are sold in batches of 1,000. The practice involves an organizer or vote mobilizer who promises the politician 1,000 votes in exchange for 20,000 or 50,000 euros. This individual then splits the money among the people who go and vote: retirees, unemployed young people. In Campania a regional seat can cost up to 60,000 euros. In Calabria you can get by with 15,000.

In general, with 1,000 euros a *capo-palazzo* in Campania can procure fifty votes. The *capo-palazzo* (neighbourhood organizer) is a non-criminal figure who manages to convince people who do not usually go to the polls to vote for such and such politician. As proof of his vote, the voter has to show a photo of the ballot, taken with his mobile phone.

In Puglia, a vote can be worth as much as 50 euros, just as it may be in Sicily. In Gela, on the southern coast of Sicily, however, there was a courageous mayor, Rosario Crocetta, who had long been committed to battling the Mafia; when he ran for the European Parliament in 2009, the clans offered him bundles of 500 votes for 400 euros. Imagine: 400 euros for 500 votes, 80 cents per vote! There is a wire-tapping report in the file of prosecutor Roberto Di Palma relative to a 2008 operation in the province of Reggio Calabria aimed at shedding light on the relationship between the Mafia and politics in Seminara, a village in Aspromonte in which the clans are able to control the votes one by one. In the intercepted conversation, the bosses say that the slate they're supporting in the municipal elections will get 1,050 votes. At the final tally the judges counted exactly 1,056 votes.

How do the clans manage the vote? This too is simple. The organization obtains ballots that are identical to those the voter finds at the polls, through obliging poll monitors or from the printers themselves. It fills them out and keeps them. The voter who wants to sell his vote goes to the clan's people and is given a ballot already filled in. Then he goes to the polling place, presents his identification and receives a regular ballot. Once in the booth, he substitutes the clan's already filled-out ballot for the ballot he received at the polling place, putting the latter in his pocket. He leaves the voting booth and hands in the ballot pre-completed by the clan. Then he goes away. He goes back to the clan, gives them the unused ballot and receives his money. The unused ballot given to the clan is filled out and given to the next voter, who takes it, votes with it and comes back with a clean one. And will in turn be paid his silver coin: 50 euros, 100 euros, 150 or a mobile phone. Or a small job if he is lucky. In this way the clan is able to elect all the politicians it wants. Sometimes we see a politician on television and we think: 'He can't speak well, doesn't have the right skills, how on earth did he get elected?' This is how he got elected.

With things the way they are, it's easy to convince yourself that they will never change, that it's hopeless to strive to make that happen, since you will never be able to shape the country's destinies. But the truth is exactly the opposite: things work that way because we don't participate, because we don't make an effort, because we don't try to effect change.

One of the things that hurts me the most is being accused of defaming my country simply because I talk about its contradictions. A person who talks about his own country is not defaming it, he's defending it. When he was Prime Minister, Silvio Berlusconi said:

If I catch whoever made the nine series of *La Piovra* and the people who write books about the Mafia [. . .], I swear I'll strangle them.

And on a later occasion:

There was publicity given to this criminal organization [. . .] let's remember the nine series of *La Piovra* and all the literature, the cultural promotion, *Gomorrah* and all the rest.

Cultural promotion? How is that conceivable? The former Prime Minister does not understand that to tell stories is to reshape the country's dream. Telling stories is already a step forward in terms of doing, because words are actions. Which is why putting a stop to words means to stop doing. Telling how things are means not having to submit to them.

I am obsessed with telling stories. I like to tell them because I like to listen to them. I have often told stories to dispute others that I didn't like. Narration has a duty: to express a point of view, which can be shared or detested. You can agree or disagree, but you can't come away from a story with every imaginable position in your head. What you do when you tell a story is choose. A monologue, a book, is a place where you propose an idea to others, who accept or reject it. It is not a place where you sound any and all conceivable notions, because in the end, if you do that, you haven't told any story or put forth any viewpoint.

I have always been struck by the questions that I am asked abroad. How can words represent a danger to criminal organizations? Isn't that an exaggeration? How can a vulnerable man like you frighten the clan? But it's not the writer himself who scares them, it's the scores of people listening, those who read a story, the numerous languages in which the story is told. The word becomes the premise of the action and, in many cases, the action itself. That's the power of stories, which has always given me faith and kept me from feeling crushed by sorrow, even when I tell a story like that of vote-buying or the love between Mina and Piergiorgio Welby.

There is a story that my grandfather Carlo always told me, a story drawn from the Jewish tradition. In the world, in every generation, there are always thirty-six just men. They don't know who they are and no one else knows who they are. But when evil seems to prevail, they rise up against it. And this is one of the reasons why God does not destroy the world. That's why understanding and recognizing wrong and trying to change it has always seemed to me to be an act of great hope. The idea that you can save the world by doing even simple things, or things considered simple, has always filled me with joy. It is a way of saying to anyone who is listening: if I do my job well this morning, I'm saving the whole world. It's like saying: this is my problem too, it concerns me, like Calamandrei's ship.

There is a poem by Borges, entitled 'The Just', which sums this all up:

A man who cultivates his garden, as Voltaire wanted.

Someone who is grateful that there is music on this earth.

One who tracks down an etymology with pleasure.

Two workers in a café in the South, enjoying a silent game of chess.

A potter envisioning a colour and shape.

The typographer who sets this page, though he may not like it.

A man and a woman reading the final tercets of a certain canto.

A person caressing a sleeping pet.

Someone who justifies a wrong done to him, or wants to.

Who is thankful for Stevenson's existence.

Who would rather that others be right.

Such people, without knowing it, are saving the world.

Epilogue

Self-Portrait of a Boss

'There's treasure buried beneath the ground in Scampia. A treasure-trove of precious stones: emeralds, topazes, rubies, lapis lazuli. And diamonds. Diamonds in particular. They put all the stones in Coke bottles, the plastic kind, big ones and little ones. I'm telling the truth; I'm not talking crazy.'

I don't bat an eye at this revelation. Then I ask the boss: 'And where is this treasure hidden? Where exactly?'

'If I knew, I would tell the magistrates. But you have to look for it: it's there, in some hole that's been dug somewhere, in places scattered around, here and there. Because I saw them with my own eyes, the Di Lauro guys: they would go to their place on Via Cupa dell'Arco, then return with the stones. Some so big they wouldn't fit in the neck of the bottle. You could pave the Naples–Rome autostrada with Paolo Di Lauro's diamonds . . .'

Speaking with me is Maurizio Prestieri, Camorra boss of Rione Monterosa, a district in Secondigliano. One of the bosses of the board that used to govern the Secondigliano Alliance.

'Italian drug traffickers now buy mainly precious stones to launder money. They have a value that never depreciates. In fact, their value increases continuously, you can hide them easily, and for liquidity you have no problem selling them anywhere in the world. Houses, cars, villas, those can be seized. Bills can be hidden in hollow walls, but after a while they get moldy and deteriorate. But diamonds . . . it's like the ad said, they're forever.'

According to the indictment, Maurizio Prestieri, Paolo Di Lauro's right-hand man, ordered about thirty killings. But primarily he is part of the story of organized crime that has made the Italian *cosche* (clans) the prime investors in the cocaine market. They thought transforming an elite drug into a mass-market drug was the future. When Prestieri is arrested in June 2003, he is a wealthy boss. He is in Marbella with his family, in the country that is a second, if not the first, home for all the European criminal organizations: Spain. After four years in prison he unexpectedly decides to cooperate, and to this day his statements in all the trials have been considered credible and truthful. His story has even been made into a book. One of the Neapolitan anti-mafia prosecutors who handles his collaboration is Luigi Alberto Cannavale: with writer Giacomo Gensini, Cannavale co-authored a passionate narrative, *I Milionari*, inspired by the affairs of the Secondigliano clan and in particular Prestieri, who in the novel based on a true story is renamed Cavani. The book describes his rapid rise and slow, painful fall in a stark, matter-of-fact style. A story that many readers will prefer to believe is false, invented, pure fiction. Because if you are a person who lives and breathes indignation, knowing that these stories are true makes you lose sleep at night.

Maurizio Prestieri is – was – a boss. He comes from one of the families defeated in the Secondigliano feud of 2004–6, though at the time he begins collaborating the Prestieri are still strong and have a solid economic structure. After the first confessions, the clan offers him a million euros for every single declaration he will recant. A ton of money to put an end to his cooperation with the law. But Prestieri doesn't stop. In fact, he also denounces this attempt at bribery. He doesn't feel like being a boss anymore. 'I'll always be who I am. What I did can't be erased. But I can act differently now.' We meet several times in a barracks. A secret place. An approximate time. You can arrive much earlier or much later. At each meeting, Maurizio Prestieri is always elegant and tanned. Grey or black pinstripe suit, ankle boots, expensive watch. No sign of the negligence that usually happens to people who have lost their power and live in hiding, like rats.

'Do you remember me?' he asks. 'I told you to go to hell, once . . . but now I've changed.' I have no idea what he's referring to. But '*O' sicco*', the 'scarecrow' as they call him in Naples, remembers. 'You were at a trial, my mother was blowing me kisses, but you thought that little old lady was sending them to Paolo Di Lauro. So you gestured as if to say, "Who is that woman, what does she want?" And I told you to go to hell . . .'

The Boss

Maurizio Prestieri is one of those bosses who rose up from nothing. Rione Monterosa, a district of Secondigliano, is where he came full circle:

> With my first profit made from a little drug dealing, I decided to do what no one in my area had ever done: fly. I told everyone: I'm taking a plane. I would be the first in my family and the first in my neighbourhood to get on one. I went to Capodichino and bought a ticket on a domestic flight. I didn't care about the destination, I just wanted it to be a place as far away from Naples as possible. And the place farthest from Naples for all of us was Turin. I took the plane, all excited. I landed, got off, walked around the airport and outside a bit, and went right back. When I returned, everyone in the area was there cheering. I felt like Gagarin, the first guy in space. I was the first person from Secondigliano to get on a plane. Everyone kept asking me: '*O' sicco*, is it true that the contraption takes you above the clouds?

The poverty in the outer localities becomes a blind, dizzying engine that enables a clan structured around cocaine to take off. 'We could have been stopped immediately by the state and instead we became rich and powerful in no time. The legal economy needs our illegal money. We had skills, put to the wrong use in society . . .'

Those men for whom a Naples–Turin flight seemed like a venture into outer space are as hungry to stand out as they are ignorant about the most basic things. According to Prestieri, Raffaele Abbinante, known as *'Papele 'e Marano'*, the future boss of the secessionists, didn't even know what a cheque was when he was a kid. 'My brother paid for a batch of hashish with a cheque and *Papele* dropped it like a hot potato, saying "I want real money, what is this paper?" And now, twenty years later, he talks about the stock market, oil investments, the price of gold. He became a businessman.'

Killing School

'We became number one because nothing could stop us. We weren't afraid of anything.' The bellicose ferocity of the Secondigliano clans grows along with their ability to leverage money. The son of *Papele' e Marano* had never killed a man, he had to be taught to kill. During a feud, having numerous gunmen is not only an element of strength or pride, but also safety. Not to mention that one of your men, no matter how loyal he is, can always betray you, whereas your son, your own blood, will not. That's why there is a school for killing. 'On Via Cupa Cardone there was a guy in a white Fiat 126, dealing drugs; he was one of our men. Abbinante told his son: "Shoot him, it's easy. Go on, drain him, shoot him full of holes."' It's a term that the Camorra has borrowed directly from autopsy reports. 'So Franchino unloaded the magazine into the guy, who ended up being a sacrificial target for the kid's baptism by fire. "You see that," his father remarked, "killing is a joke, nothing to it."'

Cosimo Di Lauro had to perform the same test. Though he was the crown prince of the clan responsible for the secessionist war, he couldn't shoot. 'To make him a *boss*, they had to make him do at least one killing,' Prestieri explains. 'One day they came up with a *quaglia appojata*.' He means a sitting duck, unarmed, unmoving, unaware of being in the sights. The Camorra almost always kills people under those conditions. 'Picardi was a pusher whom the Di Lauro had decided to offer Cosimino as a target. Cosimo goes up to the pusher who expects a hello, maybe a word or two. Instead Cosimo takes out the gun, and bam, bam, bam. But he only grazes him and the pusher runs off. To make a long story short, Cosimo looked like an asshole . . .' It was forbidden to speak about this sorry display in Secondigliano.

The savagery does not end there. Today, Prestieri explains, a simple rule applies to former members of the Di Lauro clan who want to switch to the winning side of the secessionists. 'You have to kill a relative of yours, pick one and shoot him. That's the only way they'll take you into their clan, because then they're sure you're not tricking them.' Maurizio Prestieri is precise and methodical when he talks. He looks you in the eye and is not defiant. On the contrary. When you sit face to face with him you almost get a feeling of sadness. A man like him could have done so much and instead he chose to become a boss the way you'd choose to become a businessman. For the Camorra, businessman and boss are synonymous.

Coke Manager

He presents me with a maths problem concerning the white powder, a challenge as elementary as it is mind-boggling:

When you cut a kilo of pure coke, you get about two kilos if you want the best quality, three, even four if you want low quality. A kilo of coke, including the cost of transport, reaches Secondigliano priced at 10–12,000 euros. 50–60,000 euros wholesale equates to around 150,000 euros retail: a net gain of approximately 100,000 euros. If you figure that there are outlets where up to two kilos a day are sold, working 24/7, tell me, how much do you think can be earned in a day?

The calculation is simple. If you consider that a district group can manage to handle as many as fifteen outlets, you can take in three million euros every twenty-four hours just from coke alone. I ask him about supplies. 'We would get the coke in Asturias,' Prestieri says, 'we had contacts with the Basques.' I remind him that it stirred up a hornet's nest when I reported in Spain that the Basque separatist group ETA had ties with the Camorra:

I know, they all want to make peace with the ETA, so they can't admit it. With a political organization you can sit down and negotiate, but with one mixed up in drug trafficking, what do you do? Anyway, we would buy from the Basques, Basque drug-dealers authorized and supported by the ETA. Then we stopped going there because Raffaele Amato, *'Lello o' spagnolo'*, our contact in Spain, began dealing directly with the South Americans. He had a great relationship with the guys in Cali, the Colombians who had won the war against Pablo Escobar. Here's how it works: You pay half the money for each load of coke, you remain with the Colombians as a hostage and if the other half doesn't come, they kill you. But Lello was very well treated during the period he was, let's say, sequestered. Hotels, casinos, women.

In ten years Maurizio Prestieri becomes one of the richest men in the territory and one of the most respected bosses. His family's portfolio in the periods of greatest expansion handles as much as five million euros per month. Gambling and luxury cars become his obsession. He loves Ferraris, 'but it bothered me going around Naples in my Ferrarino. Everyone looking at you, all crowding around you. It was crass. I only drove around Monte Carlo in the Ferrari.' Prestieri, unlike Paolo Di Lauro, had a talent for life. 'I knew how to live, life for me meant living each day to the fullest.

Travelling, meeting people, making money, fuck those who have it in for you. I drank in all I could of life. All the time never letting my family lack for anything and keeping them insulated from any concerns.' He floods Italy with coke but has no idea how it tastes and what sensations it produces:

> I've never used cocaine. If you wanted to be a boss in our group you couldn't use drugs. Even the Casalesi clan hold to it. To check if someone was using coke we didn't do testing or anything. We picked the guys up at night when they went home and took them to Paolo Di Lauro, then we put a plate of pasta in front of them and said 'eat'. When you snort, you have no appetite. When they didn't eat or you could tell they were forcing themselves, they were no longer trusted and were demoted. A good killer can't be a cokehead, otherwise he'll mess up. And he has to go kill on an empty stomach, for many reasons. The first is that he has to be on edge, no nodding off, and he can't afford to get the runs. The second is that if you get shot in the belly and you've eaten, you're fucked pronto. If your stomach is empty, you stand a chance of being saved.

The Ledger

The anti-mafia unit has seized dozens of ledgers. Notebooks in which the daily receipts and expenditures of the various drug outlets of the drug-trafficking network are recorded. Logs where associates enter a list of purchases each day. Like a butcher does when he opens his account book and records the names of the customers who owe him money, noting the debits and credits, that's what Prestieri's men do. In those hundreds of pages there are some disturbing entries. What throws you off is the absolute normality of it. There are figures that represent payment for utility bills, car expenses, cleaning costs for the hideouts and the houses. And then there are entries for 'Whacks', which are shootings, for 'Federico's Funeral', for the funerals of slain associates, and comments on 'crooked mechanics'. There's spending for coveralls: when a killer kills, he has to ditch his clothes. Many entries refer to 'conferences', that is, money that the clan must pay to associates' families to have them go and visit their relative in prison. Then there are entries for 'flowers for wives': even bouquets sent to wives on their birthday by incarcerated husbands, wives who are the responsibility of the clan. The amounts listed for the kilos of hashish and cocaine transacted are numerous, as are the areas from which the money comes: ZP stands for *'zona puffi'*, ZA for *'zona arco'*, ZM for *'zona monterosa'*, the various drug-dealing markets. There is no lack of strange acronyms, such as ME or LO, which stand for *Merda* or *Lota*, shit or grease, the money to be shelled out to the police monthly to avoid inspections or arrests. And a number of lawyers are listed as 'salaried attorney': they're on the clan's payroll.

Carnage

As a boy Maurizio was not destined to become a boss. He might have become the family's investor, given his entrepreneurial skills. The group's *bosses* were his brother Rosario and his older brother Raffaele in particular. Charismatic, unflappable, Raffaele enjoyed Paolo Di Lauro's complete trust, more so than a blood relation. Except that the Prestieri brothers end up in a war against a district boss whom the clan had stripped of power, taking advantage of his forced stay in Tuscany: Antonio Ruocco, known as Capaceccia. One of the most vicious feuds ever seen on Italian territory. In a series of executions, dozens of men from the two bands are killed, until Ruocco shows up at the Fulmine bar in Secondigliano on 18 May 1992, with a command of eight men: with machine guns, pistols, pump-action rifles and hand grenades they kill five people. Among them is Maurizio's older brother Raffaele, the *boss*, and Rosario, the other brother. Di Lauro, known as *Ciruzzo o' milionario* (the millionaire), stops thinking rationally and orders the kind of execution that mafia rules prohibit: the killing of Ruocco's mother. 'The clans throughout Italy let us know that they had not condoned it, but Paolo Di Lauro's response was: "This is my way of waging war."'

So Prestieri becomes a boss:

> We were able to take everything. Restaurants, bars, hotels, houses in half the world. Factories, shops, contracts. When Naples started the extension project in the area to the north, we blocked the concrete mixers to get them to award the contracts to our businesses. We would shove a .38 in the drivers' faces, make them get out and we'd take the trucks. We stopped the in-transit mixers and the cement dried inside them. That way the company lost the cement, lost the mixer-truck, which could only be scrapped, and also lost the contract because the job was delayed. At that point the contract had to be awarded to us. Coke, contracts, politics, that's how you control people's lives.

Politics? 'Politics, sure. Take good notes. These are stories that may seem unbelievable. But they're just everyday reality ... political reality.'

Grand Hotel Camorra

Italy is a country for old men, whereas the Camorra invests in young people. An older leader of a clan knows he must hand over his authority to someone else: his experience will live on, not by clinging to his own power, but by selecting the young man to whom he will transfer it. Moreover, he will save his skin if he realizes this before the younger man bumps him off and grabs that power for himself.

Maurizio Prestieri soon became Paolo Di Lauro's chosen one: he became the Secondigliano boss's favourite because he was the brother of Raffaele, Di Lauro's best friend, who'd been killed. And because he was sharp, determined, skilful. Paolo Di Lauro had never wept, or at least never in front of anyone. Once in Barcelona, a place where all the world's clans made investments and purchased coke, they were strolling along, watching a sunset, when Paolo Di Lauro said to Prestieri: 'Raffaele would have loved this sunset . . .' And he burst into tears.

The boss capable of ordering the execution of the elderly mother of one of his enemies, of not seeing his children for years in order to better manage his trafficking, wept for forty minutes straight at the sight of a sunset and the thought of a friend who had died young. Today, when I meet Prestieri in a place protected by my own security detail and the one he's had for the past three years, since he began cooperating with the law, he recalls: 'I had never seen *Ciruzzo 'o milionario* like that.'

Their relationship becomes very close. Prestieri's standing soon becomes clear to all. Once, when Maurizio has a high fever that won't come down, Di Lauro goes to his house. Worried, the boss shows up unexpectedly, knocks on the door, goes in and lies down next to him. As they talk, the boss falls asleep right there in the bed beside his friend Maurizio Prestieri. When the other guys in the clan hear about it, they begin to envy Maurizio more than anyone else: he's had the privilege of sleeping with the boss. 'And that scared me. In Naples a man can die from envy. I think we must be the most envious people in Italy. To be okay with it, Neapolitans always have to feel it's luck that allows you to obtain a thing: not commitment or ability. I was afraid of envy.'

The boss and his heir apparent were as close as father and

son. Having lost his father very early on, and then his brothers, Maurizio grew up with Paolo Di Lauro. Di Lauro raised him, believed in him, trusted him, and considered him the real brains of the group. Even today when Prestieri talks about Di Lauro, you hear a clear note of respect in his voice. 'I love him. Now he despises me. As well he should.' But back then Paolo Di Lauro puts him on a pedestal: when the boss begins to tire of his fugitive life, always hiding, always isolated from the action, he begins to give more power to Prestieri, to delegate responsibility. For a Camorra boss you are a man if you have a family; you don't divorce, but you have a lot of women. If you divorce, you are not a man. If you don't have mistresses, you are not a man.

Until then Ciruzzo had hardly ever had lovers. He had fathered ten children over the course of a long marriage of more than thirty years. 'Providence had sent him all males and this was another sign that he was destined to command. He was sure he had enough "princes" to result in generations of drug traffickers to come.'

Instead, that's where the clan's downfall began. Di Lauro's sons were incapable of running the empire, and all the clan managers rebelled:

While the authorities were looking all over the world for him, he was hiding at Castel dell 'Ovo. Yeah, right in the middle of Naples. They looked everywhere, and he was in Naples, on a yacht of ours. He was hiding out at sea. Though even in Greece and Russia the mafia families protected him. But I knew he wanted to get out of those hideouts, to stop living like a monk, nothing but kids and cocaine. So I took him with me to Slovenia. And there Ciruzzo changes: he falls in love with a gorgeous Russian girl. And does crazy things for her: he follows her to Russia, and when she disappears and goes to Geneva, while law enforcement throughout the world is looking for him, Paolo

Di Lauro risks arrest and goes to her by train, searches for her in the streets where the area's Russians lived, stations himself below her house like a lovesick adolescent willing to do anything to win back his girl.

Those are the clan's golden years, since by then, along with the Calabrians, it controls the coke economy in Italy and all over Europe. More and more the bosses live abroad:

Slovenia is paradise for us. There we find everything we'd want the world to be like. No rules. Casinos, women, friends from all over the planet. And you can buy everything and get anything you want. We would stay as long as nine months. I returned every two weeks to check Di Lauro's affairs, while Ciruzzo didn't give a fuck. He didn't go back even for New Year's. He forgot all about his sons. We felt so secure in Slovenia that we had people call us by our names. Finally, no phony documents, none whatsoever. After all, the institutions there are bought by various mafias: the Russians, the Serbs, us, the Calabrians, the Sicilians, the Casalesi clan, the Turks. All of them.

Italy is surrounded by a number of nations that the organizations consider easy territories, where the state is very weak, where it's simple to invest and where there is no anti-mafia culture: Albania, Greece, Slovenia, Croatia, Montenegro. 'I'm not someone who understands economic crises, but I can assure you that for years Paolo Di Lauro invested millions and millions of euros in Athens and on the Greek coast. Restaurants, hotels, condominiums and even industries. All the cartels invested there for years. This stymied those countries' economy, it was as if they were colonized . . . I think that to understand the crisis you'd have to start with these facts. But I'm no expert . . .'

The guys from the Secondigliano clan spend months in galactic hotel-casinos, closing business deals and having a good time at the green-felt tables. They make fortunes and squander most of them. 'One time at the casino the manager – he was an American – goes up to Paolo Di Lauro and asks: Paolo, how come you're not playing? The only card game I know is *scopa*, Ciruzzo replies. The owner laughs as if to say, what an ignorant *cafone* (peasant). Di Lauro tells him, sit down and play with me, if you win I'll give you two million euros on the spot, if you lose you give my men two million euros worth of drinks. The owner stopped laughing and said goodbye.'

In the end Italian bosses are clear about two things: people care about money and their lives. If these two things don't matter to you, or you act like you don't care about them, well then, you're already on your way to becoming a boss and controlling others. You're preparing yourself not to be afraid of anything. Prestieri was like that. He never wore clothes that cost less than ten thousand euros, but today he's quick to point out that they were classy clothes in any case:

We lived life to the fullest. I remember the most expensive dinner in my life. There was me, Vincenzo and Paolo Di Lauro and Lello Amato. A seafood restaurant, champagne and everything. We spent 12 thousand euros. Yet we could also be animals. Just think, once we're going to a club in Rimini: the whole group of clan leaders. Make sure you dress well, I tell them. And they show up wearing shoes without socks and Bermuda shorts. Nobody can stop us, they think. But you should have dressed decently, I tell them, they won't let us in here looking like that. And Gennaro Marino 'Mckay' says: '*O' sicco*, I paid 700 euros for these shoes.' 'They sure as hell aren't going to ask you for a receipt, Mckay, they look at how you're dressed,' I shoot back. Obviously the bouncers wouldn't let them in and I had to stop them before they could come out with 'maybe you don't know who you're dealing with . . .,' which wouldn't have ended well.

Prestieri had always frequented the circles of actors, singers and soccer players in Naples: the key that opened every door was cocaine. 'Once I brought cocaine to a Neapolitan actor's villa, as much as they wanted, and all the girls, the guys, the actors, everybody wanted to be my friend. I felt I had won the confidence of all the well-heeled folks in the city, me, who came from the part of Naples they considered shitty. The white stuff from the shitty part of town was different though, they liked that a lot.'

Prestieri lost a lot of money at the casino. 'I played with a little table on the side so I could eat. I never stopped playing. Only for a minute or two to go to the bathroom.' All the gamblers remember Maurizio Prestieri, especially enthusiasts of Chemin de fer, the game that made him lose and win mountains of money:

> Once there was a Ferrari at stake, the one who won the most consecutive rounds rose to the top on a giant screen in the centre of the casino, and my name was first among all the players. It was just for the fun of winning because I already had three Ferraris. Then a Neapolitan guy like me scores seven coups in a row. In a minute he catches up to me. I bank 230 thousand euros, and he throws in 230 thousand euros. Then he gets to 730 thousand euros, he doesn't let up, and I wind up leaving 750 thousand euros in the Sabot. So I lose a Ferrari and a million euros in little more than a minute.

The Casino stories are endless. In these places you're trained to burn money and consider it all a roulette, to feel cocky and powerful because you're showing everyone that you can wager sums equivalent to a company's profits. With the money they want to buy anything, even women:

> I remember there was a *soubrette* who hosted the opening of the casino season: one of the most gorgeous, well-known personalities in Italy. She was always on TV, a guest on all the programmes.

My right-hand man was nuts about her. So I tell him, go offer her 50 thousand euros and she'll sleep with you, you'll see. He says to me: *O' sicco*, are you sure? Yeah, go on, fuck off, I tell him. He goes away and comes back whipped. I looked like such an asshole, he says. When I offered her the money she looked at me in disgust and said: 'Don't you dare try that again.' So then I tell him: but you have to let her see the chips in your bag, otherwise she'll think you're just a big talker. Go on, I tell him. Let her get a look at a hundred thousand euros in chips. After a while he comes back, his eyes shining: *O' sicco*, she said yes. The two of us went on gambling and since we kept winning, he had a gorgeous Russian at his side and no longer cared about the showgirl. But we had promised her money so he went into the bedroom and only had her give him a blowjob. For a hundred thousand euros. The most expensive blowjob he ever paid for.

Prestieri comes back to the present:

Now I'm proud of the fact that I kept my kids out of all this, and I appreciate respect when it's not imposed by force and fear. When I was in the neighbourhood and drove around in the car, people would stop me and move their cars so I could park mine. Everyone greeted me and they even came after me to say hello when I didn't hear or see them, to show me that they feared me. I had a house built, spending millions and millions of euros, with a bathroom identical to the one in the Hotel de Paris. I had it furnished by the best craftsmen in Italy, the parquet alone cost a fortune. A beautiful house. Not one of those garish showcases full of gold and porcelains. Later it occurred to me that with the same money I could have bought a house in Posillipo, or in the centre of Milan, or in Piazza di Spagna in Rome. Instead I had built my palace in Secondigliano. Yet that's the logic of a Camorrista: staying put. Being boss of the compound. Nowadays, here in the North where I live, my neighbour greets me and invites me and my wife to dinner. But he doesn't know who I am. Nobody does anymore. And I'm happy that way.

The Camorra at the Ballot Box

'The Camorra controls thousands and thousands of votes. The more people turn away from politics, feeling that politicians are all the same, that they are all incapable, the more votes we are able to buy. And we were aiming to achieve a turnover in local government positions. We had a man who at the time was the youngest Italian mayor ever elected: Alfredo Cicala, mayor of Melito. Loads of articles were written about him: the young mayor of the Margherita, they called him. But he was one of ours.' The story Maurizio Prestieri tells, about the mayor of Melito, is a story that is tragically common in Campania. Cicala, after a triumphant win and a few years in office, ends up in jail, arrested for 'criminal association with the Camorra'. Assets amounting to 90 million euros are seized from him. An enormous sum for a town mayor, unthinkable that such a huge figure could be earned in such a short time and unthinkable that he could own entire condominium developments in his region unless the capital of the clans were behind it.

In this case, the money is that of the Di Lauro–Prestieri drug trade. But Cicala is not just anybody: before his arrest he engages in two parallel careers, in politics and in the clan. He becomes a member of the provincial governing board of the Margherita party and according to investigations is also able to influence the subsequent election of the Di Gennaro junta, later dissolved for mafia infiltration. Referred to as 'ò sindaco' (the mayor) by Camorra members, he is the only politician permitted to attend meetings of the bosses. Naturally he takes part in various demonstrations for the rule of law against the Camorra and Camorra members (particularly against families who are his own clan's enemies). In short, he is the perfect figure to cover up shady business and govern a territory.

The 'Nemesis' investigation of the Naples DDA (Naples District Anti-Mafia Directorate) looking into the electoral system in Melito describes the climate in the area as 'Chicago in the '30s'. Cicala becomes the clans' candidate to defeat Bernardino Tuccillo, the mayoral candidate from another branch of the centre-left. Tuccillo is well regarded, respected, determined; he's served as mayor and the Camorra tries to obstruct him in every way. It has the means to do so. 'Some candidates came to me crying,' Tuccillo said, 'begging me to tear up the forms consenting to their candidacy. Others, ashen and fearful, told me that they had had to propose their wives as candidates on the opposing party's ballot.'

One morning he found posters mourning his death posted throughout the town of Melito. He realized that it was the final warning. Like many other decent administrators in Campania, Tuccillo was abandoned by national politics. There are now many members of the local PD (Democratic Party) who supported and collaborated with Alfredo Cicala.

Prestieri knows Campania's politics well:

For politicians the Camorra becomes an honest organization during an electoral campaign, like an institution you can't do anything without. I had an office set up. An elegant office: I bought expensive antiques, archaeological pieces, notable paintings from galleries where the foremost Italian executives went to decorate their homes. And I had the upholstery made with fabrics purchased from decorators who were doing the Teatro La Fenice in Venice. In this office I received people. I gave advice, I took the names of individuals to be hired by our politicians. I heard people's complaints. If you had a problem I resolved it in my office, certainly not by going to the administration, to the non-existent counters at town hall. Here too, the Camorra is more efficient. It has a dynamic bureaucracy.

In actuality Maurizio Prestieri lived less and less in Naples and more and more in Slovenia, Ukraine and Spain. But not when there was an election around the corner. During an electoral campaign the boss's presence was required in the area:

> I come from a family that voted for the Communist Party, my father was an honest worker and when I was little he took me to all the demonstrations. I remember Berlinguer's rallies, the red flags, fists raised to the sky. But then we all became Berlusconi supporters, everybody. My clan always supported Forza Italia first, and then the Popolo della Libertà party, when they merged. I don't know how the change came about, but it was natural to align with those who want you to make money and who take all the obstacles and rules out of your way.

Prestieri knows exactly how an electoral campaign is run. Where I come from the Camorristi call the politicians '*i cavallucci*', the horses: they are merely individuals to bet on, to make them advance to the Municipality, the regional government, the Parliament, the Senate, the Government:

> Once I even served as polling place supervisor, eleven years ago. We campaign even when the polls are open, even though it's not allowed. Not only to persuade and buy those who haven't yet voted, but to be seen by the people who go to vote, as if to say: we're keeping an eye on you. Sometimes we spread the rumour that we were putting TV cameras in some of the polling places. It was nonsense, but people were intimidated and wouldn't let themselves be bought by other politicians or persuaded by some argument.

An election campaign is long but the clans are able to manage it by intimidation on the one hand and by agreement obtained through a simple trade:

> I would go and pick them up one by one. I carried infirm old women up to the polling place in my arms so they could vote. No one had ever done that. I made sure the polls in hospitals were up and running. We paid expenses for poor families, retirees' bills, the first month's rent for young couples. They all had to vote for us and we bought them cheaply. I organized bus trips for people to go vote. The clans in Secondigliano pay 50 euros per vote, and often by bribing the polling place supervisor you can more or less tell if a family of ten to fifteen people was sold to someone else. We made people feel important with a free sandwich and a paid bill. If democracy means having people participate, we are a democracy because we involve everyone. Then they vote for us and we do what we like. Contracts, drug markets, cement, investments. That's business.

Today Prestieri is almost disgusted when he talks about these things; he feels he toyed with people's souls, something that defiles you inside. And he has absolute contempt for Italian politics, like all the Camorristi. I ask him whether he had always supported the politicians of just one party. Prestieri smiles:

> We did, yes, aside from small local exceptions, like in Melito, but the Camorra divides up the territories, so it also divides up the politicians. We clashed every time with the Moccia clan who always supported the centre-left. We would celebrate the political elections when Berlusconi won and they would celebrate the municipals or regionals when Bassolino and company won. The city of Naples has always been on the left, and that was convenient for us: all those far leftists who smoked hashish and grass at Piazza Bellini or in front of the University, or who bought

coke, financed us. Freedom they said, freedom from authority, from capitalism, and then they bought tons of pot and coke. True, they voted for the left, but then we used their money to support our centre-right candidates.

I ask him whether he has ever met any centre-left politicians. 'No, never, but I'm sure that the Moccia clan together with the Licciardis endorse the centre-left, because they were our rivals and we were always talking about the division of politicians among ourselves and even with them. We were angry with them when the left won, because it meant that there was more business, more contracts, more money for them, and we had less control over what they did.'
And politicians of the centre-right, had he ever met any?

Yeah sure, I was an activist in Forza Italia and then the Popolo della Libertà for years and years. I met one of the most important figures of the PdL in Campania. I can't say his name because of the confidentiality of legal proceedings, but I remember that in March 2001, a few months before the election, this individual, followed by hordes of people, stopped at Piazza della Libertà just below my house. I was out on the balcony, enjoying the spectacle of the crowd that was following him (all our doing, since we had urged people to enthusiastically cheer him), and this politician, unconcerned about the police forces who were escorting him, started openly blowing kisses my way. I went down to meet him, and we hugged and kissed like family, while the crowd applauded the scene. I liked this because it meant that he wasn't ashamed to come to the house of a boss to ask for votes and that he regarded me as a man of power with whom he should talk. He knew very well who I was and what I did. I had already been to prison and I'd had two brothers killed in a bloodbath. He was in my neighbourhood, anyone from Naples knew whom he was dealing with when he dealt with me. At that time, however, a well-known gynaecologist came to my office, one of the luminaries of artificial insemination in Italy. When he wanted to run for mayor, he came and offered me 150 million liras in exchange for support. I couldn't accept because the clan had already picked another 'horse'.

Politicians know how to reciprocate. The strategies depend on the degree of involvement there is with the clan. If there is a direct connection, no contract will be awarded except to affiliated contractors. If instead the clan has only given 'external support', the politician will reciprocate with councilmen in key positions. Then there are the politicians who must keep their distance and are therefore limited to avoiding differences, to creating duty-free zones or generating endless construction sites to subsidize the clan and throw it a sop. 'I have always felt I was an ally of Neapolitan centre-right politics. For more than ten years I even had a disabled permit, obtained because I was an active supporter of the PdL. In the jargon of the Camorra, those passes are called *il mongoloide* (the Mongoloid). With that I parked wherever I wanted to, on car-free ecological Sundays I could drive around a deserted Naples. Fantastic!'

The Di Lauro-Prestieri clan, in control of coke, in control of local government politics, becomes more and more prosperous and finds new areas for investment: starting with China, where it enters the counterfeit market for investments in finance. There was the problem of managing the money, recycling it, investing it. 'Enzo, one of Paolo Di Lauro's sons, had a way with computers and could move money from one place to another in no time. And I was surprised once at a meeting of ours, when they talked about buying a packet of Microsoft shares. They had a man in Switzerland, Pietro Virgilio, who acted as their collector with the banks. Without Swiss banks we wouldn't have existed.'

But the fact is that the clan's rise is actually the cause of its fall. Everything seems to change when national attention is turned on them, and that happens because the clan is now travelling more and more, between Switzerland, Spain and Ukraine, and Di Lauro delegates everything to his sons. The latter take away the autonomy granted to the local bosses, whom their father had regarded as independent operators. The sons do away with the local boss's capital and decision-making authority and place them on salary. Things fall apart. A fierce war breaks out, a bloodbath in which there are as many as four killings per day. 'I always say it: we shouldn't have been VIPs, but VILPs.' VILP? What's that? I ask. 'Yeah, the L stands for Local.' Very Important Local Person! The important thing is to be important only in that territory:

> The most serious harm you journalists did by writing about the Camorra was giving them too much attention. That's the problem. If you're a VILP in Scampia, you can shoot, sell cocaine, scare people, own a trendy bar, have women look at you because you're intimidating: in short, you're a big shot. But if you shine the spotlight of all of Italy on me, the national notoriety is likely to cause the local reputation to crack, because for Italy I'm a criminal and that's that. Attention exposes me, it says I'm a violent thug, a guy who conducts dirty business; even magistrates and the police are forced to take swift action, and there are no bribes to protect you anymore.

Although Prestieri decided to cooperate, he does not speak of himself as a *pentito*, literally someone who repents, but as a soldier who betrayed his army. 'No, I'm not repentant, it would be too easy to use that to erase what I've done. Today I'm just a dirty uniform of the Camorra.' Nevertheless he feels the weight of what he did:

> The innocent killings my group performed have stayed with me. One in particular. There was a guy who was hassling our contractors, imposing hirings, stealing their cement. We had to kill him but we didn't know his name. Only where he lived. So someone

who knew his face stationed himself near the house with two hit-men. He was to shake hands with the victim: that was the signal. An hour goes by, nothing, two hours pass, nothing, then a guy comes out and goes to shake hands with our man; the shooters immediately fire, but our spotter yells *'nunnn'è iss, nunn'è iss*, it's not him!!' Too late. Not only is the young man dead, but then everyone starts saying that he was a Camorrista, because the Camorra never makes a mistake. Only we knew that wasn't it. We knew and so did his mother, who screamed herself hoarse insist-ing that her son was innocent. Nobody in Naples ever believed her. Morally I will do whatever I can in the coming months to bring justice to this young man, in the trials.

Anyone who joins a criminal organization knows what's in store for him. Prison and death. But Prestieri hates prison. He is not a boss used to living on the run in dives, always hiding, always armoured. He's used to the good life. And most likely this too motivates him to collaborate with the law. 'Prison is hard. Espe-cially in Italy. We all hoped to be incarcerated in Spain. There once a month, if you behave well, you can be with a woman, and there are gyms and activities in the jail. If you offered me ten years in Spain or five here in Poggioreale, I'd take ten in Spain.' Just as Casalesi contractors built the prison of Santa Maria Capua Vetere in Caserta, so the prison in Secondigliano was built by contractors chosen by the Secondigliano clans:

They had us visit the site before it was handed over. And we joked about it. *O' cinese*, here's where you'll end up. *O' Sicco*, this cell already has your name on it. We visited the prison where each of us would later wind up. I've spent more than ten years in prison, and there was never a day when I made the bed. When you're a boss in the Italian Mafia, in whatever prison they send you to, there's always someone who will make your bed, cook for you, trim your nails and your beard. In jail, if you're nobody, it's tough.

In the end though we all hate being in prison and we're all afraid. With my own eyes I saw Vallanzasca – a legend, since you don't usually see mafiosi from the north – practically kiss the guards' hands. Poor guy, he had an utterly shitty life in jail, he was totally under the guards' thumbs. And I said to myself, is this the legendary Vallanzasca everyone feared? This guy who stands at attention, hands behind his back, as soon as a jailer comes by? The truth is, after ten years in prison you're a lamb: we all tremble when we hear them coming, the Mobile Operative Group, that is, called in to beat us up when something goes wrong in there.

I ask Prestieri the final question, and it is the usual question that talk-show hosts pose to former criminals. Laughingly I do an impression: 'What would you say to a kid who wants to become a Camorrista?' Prestieri laughs too but with some bitterness:

I can't teach anybody anything. There are many reasons why someone becomes a Camorrista, and among them poverty is often just an excuse. I have my life, my tragedy, my failures, my family to defend, and my sins to atone for. I am only happy about one thing, that my children are studying at the university, far removed from this world. Decent kids, the only clean thing in my life.

References

1. I Swear

Ginsborg, Paul. *Salviamo l'Italia*. Einaudi, Turin 2010.

Mazzini, Giuseppe. *Dei doveri dell'uomo*. Rizzoli, Milan 2010.

Montanelli, Indro. *L'Italia del Risorgimento*. Rizzoli, Milan 1972.

Rossi, Lauro. *Mazzini e la Rivoluzione napoletana del 1799*. Piero Lacaita Editore, Manduria 1995.

2. The 'Ndrangheta in the North

Carlucci, Davide and Giuseppe Caruso. *A Milano comanda la 'ndrangheta. Come e perché la criminalità organizzata ha conquistato la capitale morale d'Italia*. Ponte alle Grazie, Milan 2009.

Ciconte, Enzo. *'Ndrangheta padana*. Rubbettino, Soveria Mannelli 2010.

Ciconte, Enzo, Vincenzo Macrì and Francesco Forgione (with illustrations by Enzo Patti). *Osso, Mastrosso, Carcagnosso. Immagini, miti e misteri della 'ndrangheta*. Rubbettino, Soveria Mannelli 2010.

Gratteri, Nicola and Antonio Nicaso, *Fratelli di sangue. Storie, boss e affari della 'ndrangheta, la mafia più potente del mondo*. Arnoldo Mondadori Editore, Milan 2010.

———. *La malapianta*. Arnoldo Mondadori Editore, Milan 2009.

Gratteri, Nicola, Antonio Nicaso and Valerio Giardina. *Cosenza 'ndrine sangue e coltelli*. Pellegrini Editore, Cosenza 2009.

Minuti, Diego and Filippo Veltri. *Lettere a San Luca*. Abramo Editore, Catanzaro 1990.

——. *Ritorno a San Luca*. Abramo Editore, Catanzaro 2008.

Oliva, Ruben and Enrico Fierro. *La Santa. Viaggio nella 'ndrangheta sconosciuta*. Rizzoli, Milan 2007.

Teti, Vito. *Il senso dei luoghi. Memoria e storia dei paesi abbandonati*. Donzelli, Rome 2004.

Veltri, Elio and Antonio Laudati. *Mafia pulita*. Longanesi, Milan 2009.

3. The Amazing Ability of the South

Fofi, Goffredo and Don Giacomo Panizza. *Qui ho conosciuto purgatorio, inferno e paradiso*. Feltrinelli, Milan 2011.

4. Waste and Contaminants: The Toxic Mountain

Baldessarro, Giuseppe and Manuela Iatì. *Avvelenati. Questa storia deve essere raccontata perché uccide la nostra gente*. Città del Sole, Reggio Calabria 2010.

Bocca, Riccardo. *Le navi della vergogna*. Rizzoli, Milan 2010.

Cordova, Claudio. *Terra venduta: così uccidono la Calabria. Viaggio di un giovane reporter sui luoghi dei veleni*. Laruffa Editore, Reggio Calabria 2010.

Corona, Gabriella and Daniele Fortini. *Rifiuti. Una questione non risolta*. Edizioni XL, Rome 2010.

De Crescenzo, Daniela.*'O Cecato. La vera storia di uno spietato killer: Giuseppe Setola*. Tullio Pironti Editore, Naples 2009.

Lucarelli, Carlo. *Navi a perdere*. Edizioni Ambiente, Milan 2008.

Sodano, Tommaso and Nello Trocchia. *La peste. La mia battaglia contro i rifiuti della politica italiana*. Rizzoli, Milan 2010.

Veltri, Elio and Antonio Laudati. *Mafia pulita*. Longanesi, Milan 2009.

V.AA. *Ecomafia 2010*. Edizioni Ambiente, Milan 2010.

5. The Earthquake in L'Aquila

Arminio, Franco. *Viaggio nel cratere*. Sironi, Milan 2003.

Caporale, Giuseppe. *L'Aquila non è Kabul. Cronaca di una tragedia annunciata*. Castelvecchi Editore, Rome 2009.

Ciambotti, Sara. *Il terremoto di Sara. L'Aquila, 6 aprile, ore 3.32*. Rizzoli, Milan 2009.

Di Persio, Samanta and Ju Tarramutu. *La vera storia del terremoto in Abruzzo*. Casaleggio Associati, Milan 2009.

Erbani, Francesco. *Il disastro. L'Aquila dopo il terremoto, le scelte, le colpe*. Laterza, Rome-Bari 2010.

Puliafito, Alberto. *Protezione civile Spa. Quando la gestione dell'emergenza si fa business*. Aliberti Editore, Reggio Emilia 2010.

VV.AA. *Ecomafia 2010*. Edizioni Ambiente, Milan 2010.

6. The Mudslinging Machine

Caponnetto, Antonino. *Io non tacerò. La lunga battaglia per la giustizia*. Maria Grimaldi, ed., Melampo, Milan 2010.

Caselli, Gian Carlo. *Le due guerre. Perché l'Italia ha sconfitto il terrorismo e non la mafia*. Melampo, Milan 2009.

Chiaromonte, Gerardo. *I miei anni all'antimafia 1988–1992*. Calice Editore, Rome 1996.

Deaglio, Enrico. *Il raccolto rosso 1982–2010. Cronaca di una guerra di mafia e delle sue tristissime conseguenze*. Il Saggiatore, Milan 2010.

De Cataldo, Giancarlo. *Terroni*. Sartorio Editore, Pavia 2006.

Fava, Claudio. *I disarmati. Storia dell'antimafia: i reduci e i complici*. Sperling & Kupfer, Milan 2009.

La Licata, Francesco. *Storia di Giovanni Falcone*. Feltrinelli, Milan 2005.

Monti, Giommaria. *Falcone e Borsellino. La calunnia, il tradimento, la tragedia*. Editori Riuniti, Rome 2006.

Patrono, Mario. *Il cono d'ombra*. Cerri Editore, Milan 1996.

7. Piero and Mina

De Septis, Elisabetta. *Eutanasia.* Messaggero di Sant'Antonio, Padua 2008.

Fornero, Giovanni. *Bioetica cattolica e bioetica laica.* Bruno Mondadori, Milan 2009.

Furlanetto, Flavia. *Una vita vissuta dalla porta d'uscita. Paolo Ravasin e la Sla.* Sangel Edizioni, Cortona 2010.

Milano, Gianna and Mario Riccio. *Storia di una morte opportuna. Il diario del medico che ha fatto la volontà di Welby.* Sironi, Milan 2008.

Welby, Mina. *Pino Giannini, L'ultimo gesto d'amore.* Edizioni Noubs, Chieti 2010.

Welby, Piergiorgio. *Lasciatemi morire.* Rizzoli, Milan 2006.

Welby, Piergiorgio and Francesco Lioce, ed. *Ocean Terminal.* Castelvecchi Editore, Rome 2009.

8. Democracy Bought and Sold and the Ship of the Constitution

Calamandrei, Piero. *La Costituzione e la gioventù. Discorso pronunciato da Piero Calamandrei nel gennaio 1955 a Milano.* Provincia di Livorno, Livorno 1975.

——. *Elogio dei giudici scritto da un avvocato.* Ponte alle Grazie, Florence 1993.

——. *In difesa dell'onestà e della libertà della scuola.* Sellerio, Palermo 1994.

——. *La Costituzione e leggi per attuarla.* Giuffré, Milan 2000.

——. *Ada con gli occhi stellanti. Lettere 1908–1915.* Sellerio, Palermo 2005.

——. *Fede nel diritto.* Laterza, Roma-Bari 2008.

——. *Per la scuola.* Sellerio, Palermo 2008.

Constitution of the Italian Republic, Part I, Rights and Duties of Citizens, Title II, Ethical and Social Rights and Duties, Art. 34. https://www.senato.it/documenti/repository/istituzione/costituzione_inglese.pdf

Acknowledgements

Words are always the result of encounters and clashes, hours of silence and deafening noise. The words in this book were generated in a garage. And I don't mean in a figurative sense. The stories, the lists, the ideas were born to the sound of flooded engines in need of repair, spurts of water to hose away grease and oil, and bursts of air for inflating tires. Our editorial office was literally in a car wash, on the first floor of a garage in Milan where, for security reasons, we were virtually locked up.

My thanks to everyone who worked with me on the original TV programme, who defended it from the start, and to Loris Mazzetti, who paid for his efforts to keep us on the air by being handed a suspension. My thanks to Roberto Benigni, who was the first to support this project. My thanks to all the guests who experienced this adventure with me.

My thanks to the prosecutors, and to the Carabinieri Territorial Group in Locride, for guiding me through a very beautiful and terrifying land.

My thanks, as always, to those who have been watching over my life for years now, the fourteen men who make up my guard detail: Gaetano, Roberto, Claudio, Nicolò, Giuseppe, Rosario, Giuliano, Vittorio and others, who agreed to spend a long time away from home, with a smile and with a great deal of discipline, in support of my work.

My thanks to everyone who made the realization of this project possible; listing them all would be challenging, since they are truly so numerous. And to those who remained close to me through the most difficult times. Thanks to my English publisher, who believes in me and my work. Thanks to Anne Appel, who made my words yours.

And thanks to my family, who are subjected to pressure, isolation and suffering, but endure it.